RAISING CAPITAL
WITH CONFIDENCE

RAISING CAPITAL

WITH CONFIDENCE

DARIN H. MANGUM, ESQ.

ISBN: 978-1-78324-349-5 (paperback)
ISBN: 978-1-78324-355-6 (hardback)

Published by Wordzworth
www.wordzworth.com

For Shannon,
Your belief in me has been the foundation of everything I do.

TABLE OF CONTENTS

FOREWORD

It's an honor to contribute a foreword to Darin Mangum's substantial work, *Raising Capital with Confidence*. Having an extensive background in the startup ecosystem, I deeply appreciate the complexity and nuance involved in raising capital, especially within the rapidly changing financial and legal landscapes entrepreneurs face today.

Darin Mangum, a distinguished securities attorney and someone whom I've had the pleasure of collaborating with, is certainly one of the most insightful voices when it comes to navigating these very challenges. His profound understanding of securities law is paralleled only by his commitment to ensuring entrepreneurs are well-equipped to meet the demands of legal compliance while pursuing innovative pathways to business funding.

His book distills years of his professional wisdom and practical insights into a guide that is not only accessible but also empowering for entrepreneurs, whether they are just embarking on their first fundraising journey or seeking advanced strategies in alternative securities options. Darin's ability to demystify complex legal terms into actionable strategies is truly commendable and serves as a beacon of clarity in the dense fog of securities issuance and capital acquisition.

What sets *Raising Capital with Confidence* apart is its dual focus on legal diligence and strategic creativity, guiding business owners through the intricate pathways of private placements, crowdfunding laws, and the burgeoning field of digital securities. Darin seamlessly integrates real-world scenarios with straightforward expert advice, making it an indispensable resource for today's innovative entrepreneurs who dream of reaching new heights of success.

As someone deeply entrenched in the startup world, I believe that this work is a vital tool for anyone committed to not only raising capital but doing so with the assurance of legal compliance and market confidence. It's a guide that helps align the nascent potential of entrepreneurship with the structured discipline of law, thereby paving a clearer path to sustainable business growth.

In *Raising Capital with Confidence*, you'll discover not just the how, but also the why behind modern capital-raising practices, thanks to Darin's enriching explanations and comprehensive approach. I wholeheartedly recommend this book to every entrepreneur aiming to secure their future in the competitive business arena.

Lastly, in the broader business context, remember that engaging with professionals—such as experienced legal counsel and consultants—can further bridge the gap between innovative business ideas and practical execution, ensuring that your ambitions are matched with strategies that resonate with both market realities and regulatory requirements.

Sincerely,

John Richards
Provo, Utah

FOUNDER OF STARTUP IGNITION
ENTREPRENEUR | VENTURE INVESTOR | MENTOR | ADVISOR

PREFACE

Over the past 25 years, I've had the privilege of working with a diverse range of entrepreneurs, start-ups, and investment companies around the globe. As managing partner of Mangum & Associates, a boutique securities law firm I founded in 1999, I've helped guide clients through the complex process of raising capital.

Through these experiences including raising capital for a number of my own personal ventures from time to time, I've seen firsthand the challenges businesses face when navigating the intricate landscape of securities law and the private and public capital markets.

Raising Capital with Confidence is a reflection of the knowledge I've gained from years of working with clients across industries, from private equity funds and venture capital firms to blockchain and cryptocurrency issuers.

My goal in writing this book is to demystify what I often call the "alphabet soup" of securities regulations and the capital-raising process with a view toward providing entrepreneurs, business owners, and executives with the tools they need to approach it with confidence and clarity.

The reality is that raising capital is not just about finding the right investors or securing the largest investment; it's about navigating regulatory compliance, structuring deals that benefit both the business and investors, and understanding the nuances of different capital-raising strategies. From real estate syndications to technology start-ups, every business faces its own unique challenges, but the common thread is the need for strategic, informed guidance.

All too often, I've witnessed poor souls who "do it wrong" and find themselves in the crosshairs of securities regulators facing securities fraud charges. The best ideas and businesses can quickly go down the tubes if you don't "do it right."

In addition to my role at Mangum & Associates, I also serve as CEO of ZuLoo, Inc., a benefit corporation focused on tackling the global sanitation crisis through innovative social enterprise. This work has further reinforced my belief that with the right approach, capital can be raised not only for profit but also for a positive impact on the world.

Whether you are a first-time entrepreneur or an experienced business owner seeking new ways to raise capital, this book will provide you with insights and practical strategies drawn from real-world examples. It is my hope that you'll find the knowledge within these pages helpful as you embark on your own capital-raising journey.

Remember, while this book offers valuable information, every capital raise is unique. I encourage you to seek professional advice whether from a seasoned securities attorney or financial advisor to ensure you are making informed decisions at every step of the way.

Thank you for taking the time to explore this critical topic. I wish you all the best in raising capital for your business.

Sincerely,

Darin H. Mangum, Esq.
San Juan, Puerto Rico

INTRODUCTION

Raising capital is one of the most critical and often daunting tasks that entrepreneurs, business owners, and executives face. Whether you're just starting a business or looking to expand an established company, the ability to secure the right kind of working and growth capital can often mean the difference between success and failure. While many business owners have brilliant ideas, a solid business model, and the passion to see their vision through, raising capital requires an entirely different set of skills and knowledge. This book aims to bridge that gap.

As someone who has spent more than two decades working in the complex world of securities law and SEC regulations, I have had the privilege of guiding hundreds of clients—start-ups, venture capital (VC) funds, real estate developers, private equity firms, and more—through the capital-raising process. Throughout my career, one thing has remained clear: Raising capital is not just about finding money; it's about finding the right kind of money, in the right way, while complying with the laws that govern the process.

The landscape of capital raising has changed significantly in recent years. New regulations, alternative financing mechanisms like crowd-funding, and the rise of digital securities have created both opportunities and challenges for entrepreneurs. Traditional methods, such as private placements under Regulation D, continue to be powerful tools, but they are not one-size-fits-all solutions. The modern entrepreneur must be adaptable and strategic, carefully choosing the path that best aligns with their business goals and growth trajectory.

I wrote this book to provide a practical guide for navigating the complexities of raising capital in today's regulatory and financial environment. It is designed to be comprehensive yet accessible offering insights and strategies from my years of experience as a securities attorney. From understanding the different types of securities to knowing where to find investors and from structuring deal terms to staying compliant with federal and state securities laws, *Raising Capital with Confidence* covers the key aspects that every entrepreneur should be aware of before embarking on their capital-raising journey.

Most important, this book emphasizes that while raising capital is essential for growth, it must be done in a way that protects both the business and the investors. The decisions you make during the capital-raising process will have long-lasting implications not only for your company's financial health but also for its governance and ownership structure. By understanding your options and the associated risks, you can approach capital raising with a clearer strategy ensuring that you're building a solid foundation for long-term success.

This book is not intended to replace professional advice, and I strongly encourage you to consult with a qualified attorney, financial advisor, or other professional to tailor your approach to your specific situation. My hope is that this book will equip you with the knowledge you need to ask the right questions, avoid common pitfalls, and confidently raise the capital your business needs to thrive.

Let's get started!

CHAPTER 1

Overview of the US Private Capital Markets

Understanding the private capital markets is critical for any entrepreneur, investor, or company looking to raise capital in the United States. Raising capital in the US offers unique opportunities but comes with its own set of complexities. Unlike the public equity markets where capital is raised through securities that are traded openly, the private capital marketplace involves transactions that are not subject to the same level of public scrutiny. This chapter introduces the key aspects of private capital formation and provides a foundation for navigating this vast, intricate space. Whether you're an emerging start-up or a seasoned investor, knowing how to operate within this system is essential to securing financing while complying with US regulations.

Understanding Private Capital Formation

"Private capital formation" refers to the process of raising funds from private investors rather than through public offerings. This can take many forms, including investments from venture capital (VC) firms, private equity funds, angel investors, institutional investors, family offices, individual accredited investors, and even smaller crowdfunding investors.

What distinguishes private capital markets from their public counterparts is the nature of the investments and the transactions themselves. These deals often involve fewer regulatory disclosures, giving parties more flexibility to negotiate terms directly.

The key players in private capital markets include VC firms, private equity firms, and institutional investors such as pension funds and hedge funds. However, angel groups, family offices, individual accredited investors, and crowdfunding investors often play a critical role, especially in the early days of an enterprise. Each type of investor brings a different set of investment expectations, risk tolerances, and time horizons to the table. VCs, for example, tend to focus on early-stage companies with high growth potential, whereas private equity firms typically invest in more mature businesses, sometimes restructuring them for a future sale or public offering. In the case of many family offices, individual accredited investors or crowdfunding investors oftentimes are just looking for investment alternatives to grow their portfolios beyond the "plain toast" investment products typically pedaled by their stockbroker or investment advisor. Understanding these distinctions is vital because each investor type plays a specific role in the broader capital formation landscape.

Fundamentals of Private Capital Markets

The US capital market is divided into two main categories: public and private. While public markets are characterized by the listing of securities on exchanges such as NASDAQ and the New York Stock Exchange, the private capital markets (also referred to as the "alternative" investment space) operate outside of these exchanges. Private fundraising is a more flexible but complex process. It usually involves direct negotiations with investors and doesn't require the same public filings with the Securities and Exchange Commission (SEC) that public offerings do.

In private markets, the types of funds and structures are as varied as the industries they serve. VC, real estate development, private lending, litigation finance, hedge funds, and funds focused on distressed assets each have their own operational and legal frameworks. These structures are tailored to the risk appetite and return expectations of the investors involved. For example, VC funds typically structure investments through shares of convertible preferred stock that give them both upside potential and downside protection. Buyout funds, meanwhile, may rely more heavily on debt to finance acquisitions using the target company's assets as collateral.

Legal and Regulatory Framework

The legal environment governing the private capital markets is intricate with oversight primarily conducted by the SEC at the federal level and "blue sky" laws at the state level. One of the key regulatory frameworks affecting private fundraising is the Securities Act of 1933, which requires that securities offered in the US be registered with the SEC unless they qualify for an exemption. Common exemptions include Rule 506(b) and 506(c) under Regulation D, which allow companies to raise unlimited amounts of capital from accredited investors without going through the public registration process.

State blue sky laws also play a critical role in regulating securities offerings and require issuers to comply with additional local requirements. These laws vary by state, and noncompliance can lead to significant penalties or even legal action. Additionally, private capital raisers must adhere to rigorous disclosure requirements, which is accomplished through delivery of a comprehensive private placement memorandum (PPM), ensuring that investors have all the material information necessary to make an informed decision. Failure to meet these disclosure standards can result in severe legal consequences, including rescission rights for investors and SEC enforcement actions.

Investment Strategies

The private capital markets encompass a wide range of investment strategies tailored to different stages of a company's life cycle. Buyout funds, for example, focus on acquiring established companies through leveraged buyouts or management buyouts. In these transactions, the goal is typically to improve operational efficiency, restructure the company's balance sheet, and eventually sell it for a profit either to another company or through a public offering.

VC, by contrast, targets early-stage companies with high growth potential. These investments are inherently riskier but offer the possibility of substantial returns if the company scales successfully. VC funds often provide not only capital but also strategic guidance and networking opportunities to help start-ups grow into successful enterprises.

Another significant strategy in private capital markets is distressed investing. This approach focuses on companies facing financial difficulties often requiring restructuring or turnaround efforts. Investors in distressed assets seek to buy companies or their securities at a discount with the aim of profiting from their recovery or liquidation.

Deal Structuring and Due Diligence

Deal structuring is one of the most critical elements in the private capital markets. It involves determining the terms of the transaction, including the price, control rights, exit strategies, and protections for both investors and companies. Investors must carefully balance risk and reward while aligning the interests of all parties. Common structures include equity, debt, or hybrid instruments such as convertible debt, which provides flexibility in an investment's future.

Due diligence is a vital part of the investment process. It involves thoroughly vetting the target company's financial health, operational stability, legal standing, and growth potential. Investors perform due diligence to ensure that the company's valuation and business prospects align with the terms being negotiated. A rigorous due diligence process minimizes risk and uncovers any potential liabilities that could derail the investment later on.

Valuation Methods and Performance Measurement

Valuing private investments can be more art than science, given the lack of public market data. Different approaches such as discounted cash flow (DCF) analysis, comparable company analysis, or precedent transactions are commonly used depending on the company's stage and industry. These methods allow investors to estimate a fair market value for the target company.

In practice, and in real life, the price at which you offer investors the opportunity to invest in your company or venture ultimately is the price you're willing to accept balanced against what investors are willing to pay (i.e., how bad do you need the money vs. how eager investors are to invest).

Measuring the performance of private investments is another challenge because these investments don't offer the same level of liquidity or transparency as public markets. Common benchmarks include internal rate of return and multiple on invested capital, which provide insights into the profitability of an investment over time. Investors must also track performance metrics to ensure that their portfolio is achieving the expected returns relative to the risk taken.

In practice and in real life, the price at which you offer investors the opportunity to invest in your company or venture ultimately is the price you're willing to accept balanced against what investors are willing to pay (i.e., how bad you need the money vs. how eager investors are to invest).

Investor Relations and Fundraising

Successful fundraising in private markets often hinges on building strong relationships with investors. These relationships are grounded in trust, transparency, and consistent communication. Fund managers and company executives need to articulate their strategy clearly, providing regular updates on fund performance, market conditions, and any material changes to their investment thesis.

Fundraising strategies vary widely, depending on the type of fund and the stage of the company seeking capital. It's essential to tailor your pitch to the specific needs and expectations of your investors, whether they're high-net-worth individuals, family offices, or institutional investors. Transparency, due diligence, and preparation and delivery of a full-disclosure PPM are equally important on the investor's side to ensure that they understand the risks and potential rewards involved.

Future Trends and Challenges

The US private capital markets continues to evolve driven by regulatory changes, technological innovations, and shifting investor preferences. One emerging trend is the increasing role of technology in streamlining due diligence, deal sourcing, and even fundraising itself. Platforms like SEC-registered crowdfunding portals that connect investors with companies seeking capital are democratizing the process, making it easier for smaller businesses to access investment capital.

When our clients were raising equity investment capital for real estate development prior to the 2008 financial crisis ... promises of double-digit rates of return were commonplace.

However, the private capital landscape has its challenges. Regulatory scrutiny is likely to increase as private markets grow in size and influence. Additionally, macroeconomic factors such as interest rates, inflation, and global market conditions can significantly impact the availability and cost of capital.

For example, when our clients were raising equity investment capital for real estate development prior to the 2008 financial crisis—in 2005, 2006, and 2007—promises of double-digit rates of return were commonplace due to extremely low interest rates (and the fact that almost anyone with a pulse could get a loan). When the world thereafter proceeded to fall off a cliff and cheap debt (or bank loans of any kind) came to a screeching halt, real estate developers who didn't get wiped out had to quickly pivot paying "highway robber" interest rates to hard money lenders to keep their projects alive and often had to give up far more equity or other concessions to investors because of the shockwaves of the financial crisis that roiled the US private and public capital markets.

Needless to say, investors and companies alike must stay agile and informed to successfully navigate the complex, dynamic financial environment of our times.

CHAPTER **2**

Seven Key Considerations When Raising Capital

1. Understanding Your Capital Needs

Before embarking on any capital-raising journey, it is essential to have a clear understanding of your business's financial requirements. Assessing your capital needs is more than just estimating how much money you require; it involves a deep analysis of your company's growth trajectory, expansion plans, and strategic objectives. This step ensures you align the amount of capital raised with the actual financial demands of your business.

One of the first tasks is to evaluate the specific objectives you intend to achieve with the new funding. For instance, are you seeking capital to expand operations, acquire a parcel of real estate, develop new products, or scale your sales team? Understanding these goals will help you determine whether you need short-term bridge financing or a more substantial long-term capital injection. Additionally, the source of funding, whether it's equity, debt, or another financial instrument, must be suited to the purpose and scale of your needs.

Timing is another key factor. You need to not only consider not only when the capital is required but also the stages of capital needs. Companies often underestimate how quickly they'll need additional funds after the initial raise leading to cash flow shortages. Mapping out capital needs at each stage of growth from seed stage to Series A and beyond will allow for more strategic and less rushed capital raising.

> *I frequently advise clients to be in "always be capital raising" (ABCR) mode and to have a PPM at the ready that addresses their entire foreseeable capital needs, including contingency reserves.*

I frequently advise clients to be in "always be capital raising" (ABCR) mode and to have a PPM at the ready that addresses their entire foreseeable capital needs, including contingency reserves. A PPM can be structured in phases and adjusted as needed as you hit certain benchmarks. A PPM is an essential tool enabling you to raise capital at any time for any reason.

2. Building a Compelling Investment Case

Once your capital needs are understood, the next step is to craft a persuasive investment case that will attract potential investors. This involves not only presenting financial projections but also telling a story about why your business is an attractive investment opportunity. To do this effectively, you need to highlight your company's unique value proposition: What makes you stand out from competitors?

Your investment case should clearly articulate the unique selling points of your business. Whether it's a disruptive technology, a scalable business model, or a first-mover advantage in an untapped market, it's critical to demonstrate why investors should believe in your vision. Market potential and growth opportunities must also be emphasized because investors want to see a path to scale and profitability. You must include data-driven insights about the industry and market trends that back up your claims.

Additionally, investors look for clarity in a business model; how will your company generate revenue and sustain growth? A clear, scalable model backed by realistic assumptions is vital in securing investor confidence. Finally, you must demonstrate that the company's leadership has the experience and expertise necessary to execute the business plan effectively.

3. Targeting the Right Investors

Not all investors are created equal, and it is crucial to find the right ones for your business. The process begins by identifying investors whose profile aligns with your company's industry, growth stage, and investment criteria. Some investors specialize in early-stage ventures, whereas others prefer later-stage growth companies. Similarly, some may focus on specific sectors, such as health care or fintech, whereas others may have broader interests.

Researching and understanding investor preferences is a critical step in ensuring a good fit. Investors tend to have unique preferences when it comes to deal structure, risk tolerance, and investment horizons. By aligning your business objectives with an investor's focus areas, you increase the likelihood of securing their interest. For instance, a VC firm focused on high-growth tech start-ups would be a poor fit for a capital-intensive, asset-heavy manufacturing company.

Tailoring your investor outreach based on this research is key. Develop a target list of investors likely to share your vision whose investment objectives align with your business goals. Use your networks and professional connections to facilitate introductions; warm introductions significantly increase the chances of getting a meeting. Building relationships is just as important as pitching because investors often want to see long-term potential beyond the immediate deal.

4. Structuring the Capital Raise

The structure of your capital raise has a profound impact on your company's future, especially in terms of ownership, control, and dilution. Different financing structures, equity, debt, or hybrid models, come with their own implications, and it's vital to understand the trade-offs involved.

Equity financing, for example, involves selling shares of your company in exchange for capital. While this approach allows for significant funding without immediate repayment, it results in ownership dilution and can affect control over the company. Meanwhile, debt financing allows you to retain ownership but involves the burden of repayment with interest, which can strain cash flow.

Hybrid models, such as convertible debt, offer flexibility by allowing debt to convert into equity at a later stage often when the company's valuation has increased. The key is to align the structure with your long-term vision and exit strategy. For instance, if an initial public offering (IPO) or acquisition is your end goal, you'll need to design the capital structure to facilitate that outcome.

When structuring a capital raise, you must also consider the interests of investors. They will likely seek protections such as liquidation preferences, anti-dilution clauses, or board seats. Striking a balance between securing capital and maintaining control over your company is a delicate but essential part of the process.

5. Valuation and Investor Expectations

Determining the valuation of your company is both an art and a science. Valuation sets the stage for negotiations with investors and dictates the equity stakes or debt terms you offer. A high valuation can be attractive because it minimizes dilution, but it also sets high expectations for future growth and returns. Conversely, undervaluing your business can leave equity on the table and may signal a lack of confidence in your potential.

To assess your company's valuation, consider several factors such as the following:

- Market conditions
- Your company's financial performance
- Comparable companies in your industry
- Future growth potential

Various valuation methodologies such as DCF, comparable company analysis, and precedent transactions may be used depending on the specifics of your business.

Investors also have their own expectations regarding returns, often looking for multiples of their initial investment. For example, pitching a high-tech, long-term growth stock opportunity to an investor who is into "hard money" real estate lending and who is accustomed to doubling their money every six months will likely go nowhere and be a waste of your (and their) time. Understanding these expectations helps guide negotiations and ensures both parties are aligned. It's important to be realistic in setting expectations to avoid future disputes or disappointment. The key is to negotiate favorable terms that reflect both the current state of the business and its potential without inflating valuations beyond what the business can realistically achieve.

6. Legal and Regulatory Considerations

Raising capital comes with a myriad of legal and regulatory hurdles that must be navigated carefully. One of the most significant considerations is compliance with securities laws, particularly the Securities Act of 1933, which governs the offer and sale of securities in the US.

Pitching a high-tech long-term growth stock opportunity to an investor who is into "hard money" real estate lending and who is accustomed to doubling their money every six months will likely go nowhere and be a waste of your (and their) time.

Companies privately raising capital typically rely on exemptions from registration, such as Regulation D, which allows for capital raising from accredited investors without the full rigors of public offerings. Other exemptions such as Regulation S and Regulation Crowdfunding (Reg CF) are also paths to legal compliance.

Navigating the regulatory landscape also means understanding disclosure requirements and investor protection regulations. Missteps in this area can lead to significant legal liabilities, including penalties, fines, and the unwinding of a capital raise. Working with experienced legal counsel is indispensable to ensure that your offering documents, investor disclosures, and contractual agreements are compliant with the relevant laws.

In addition to federal regulations, state blue sky laws may impose additional requirements for companies seeking to raise capital. Failing to adhere to these local regulations can result in enforcement actions or delays in the fundraising process.

7. Pitching and Investor Relations

Your pitch is often the first impression investors have of your business, and crafting a compelling narrative is essential to capturing their interest.

A well-structured pitch deck should highlight the key elements of your investment case, including the following:

- Value proposition
- Market potential
- Business model
- Team

It's crucial to keep the presentation concise, data-driven, and visually engaging because investors often have limited time to evaluate numerous opportunities.

Effective pitching also requires honing your delivery. When presenting in front of a group investors or during a one-on-one meeting whether in-person, on a Zoom call, or in a webinar, your communication should be clear, confident, and passionate. Investors want to see that you not only understand your business but also can drive it toward success.

Beyond the initial pitch, investor relations are about building and maintaining long-term relationships. Transparency is key to this process. Keep investors informed through regular updates and progress reports, particularly regarding financial performance and milestones. Cultivating trust with your investors ensures continued support and can open doors to future fundraising rounds or strategic partnerships.

For readers who want to start taking action while reading this book, I've included the following checklist that we typically share with new clients turning the key points of this chapter into action items that may be helpful for you:

M&A
MANGUM & ASSOCIATES

Raising Capital Checklist

☐ **Hire a securities attorney**

Federal and state securities laws are serious and carry civil and criminal penalties if it's not done properly. You'll want to hire a securities attorney at least 30 days prior to pitching investors.

☐ **Gather your corporate records**

Gather all your corporate records and scan them into one electronic sharable file folder. If you haven't organized your business formally, your securities can recommend the best corporate structure and help you properly set it up prior to pitching investors.

☐ **Nail your story**

Investors love a compelling story. What's yours? What sets you apart from your competition? Of all the other deals they could invest in, why you? Why now? Be prepared to describe it in 30 seconds or less (your elevator pitch).

☐ **Define your team**

Ultimately investors don't invest in companies — they invest in people. Strong teams drive investor confidence. What is your background and relevant experience and that of your team? Going solo? No problem — but you may want to surround yourself with professional advisors to raise the credibility level of your deal.

☐ **Determine how much you need**

You don't want to run out of rocket fuel (money) halfway to the moon. Run through some possible hypothetical scenarios — the good, the bad, and the ugly — just so you know how much capital you really need.

☐ **Define your investor type**

What kind of investors do you want-- small investors, high net worth investors, or a family office or institutional "whale"? Your marketing strategy and compliance with securities laws will turn on answering these key questions.

☐ **Clarify your deal terms**

What does the investor get for their money? Running through a few hypothetical scenarios will help arrive at fair deal points. Your securities attorney will then make sure it's structured properly from a legal standpoint.

M&A
MANGUM & ASSOCIATES

America's Premier Securities Law Firm™
New York | Los Angeles | Salt Lake City | Houston | San Juan

CHAPTER **3**

Deal Terms and Types of Securities

When raising capital, entrepreneurs must understand the various types of securities that can be issued to investors. Each security has distinct characteristics, rights, and implications for both the issuer and the investor.

In this chapter, we'll explore the most common securities used in the US private capital markets providing entrepreneurs with the foundational knowledge needed to structure deals that align with their goals and those of their investors.

Types of Securities

Common Stock

Definition and Characteristics

Common stock represents ownership in a company and is the most straightforward form of equity security. Holders of common stock typically have voting rights that allow them to influence significant decisions such as electing board members or approving major corporate actions. This voting power is proportional to the number of shares owned.

Voting Rights and Ownership Implications

Common stockholders are usually entitled to one vote per share giving them a say in the governance of the company. However, in cases where a company issues multiple classes of stock, some shares may come with enhanced or diminished voting rights. For example, some founders retain "super-voting" shares to maintain control while raising capital. Ownership of common stock does not typically guarantee dividends because these payments are usually at the discretion of the company's board of directors.

Pros and Cons for Investors and Issuers

For investors, common stock offers the potential for significant capital appreciation, especially if the company experiences substantial growth. However, common stockholders are the last to be paid in the event of liquidation, making it a riskier investment compared to other types of securities. For issuers, common stock is attractive because it doesn't obligate the company to make regular payments, unlike debt. However, issuing common stock dilutes ownership and potentially cedes some control over the company.

Typical deal terms for common stock include the following:

- The number of shares issued
- Price per share
- Voting rights
- Restrictions on the transfer of shares

Anti-dilution provisions may also be included to protect early investors from future equity raises at lower valuations.

Preferred Stock

Definition and Features

Preferred stock is a hybrid security that combines characteristics of both equity and debt. While preferred shareholders do not usually have voting rights, they have a higher claim on assets and earnings than common shareholders. Preferred stock often pays a fixed dividend, making it more appealing to investors seeking regular income.

Preference in Dividend Payments and Liquidation

Preferred shareholders have priority over common shareholders when it comes to receiving dividends and recovering their investment in the event of liquidation. This preference is a key reason investors are drawn to preferred stock because it provides a level of downside protection.

Conversion Rights and Participation in Company Governance

Many preferred stock agreements include conversion rights allowing preferred shares to be converted into common stock under specific conditions such as an IPO. While preferred stockholders typically do not participate in day-to-day governance, certain events like a sale of the company may trigger special voting rights or protective provisions.

Preferred stock deals often include terms like the following:

- Dividend rates
- Liquidation preferences
- Conversion rights
- Conditions under which the stock may be redeemed or converted to common stock

Anti-dilution protections and participation rights are commonly negotiated.

Convertible Notes

Explanation of Convertible Debt Instruments

Convertible notes are debt instruments that convert into equity at a later date usually when the company raises a subsequent round of financing. This hybrid instrument allows companies to raise capital quickly without determining a fixed valuation upfront.

Conversion Mechanics and Triggers

Convertible notes typically convert into equity when the company raises a priced equity round often at a discount to the valuation of that round. The discount rewards early investors for the risk they took by investing in the note. In addition, some convertible notes come with a valuation cap limiting the price at which the note converts into equity, thereby providing early investors with a better deal.

Advantages and Considerations for Both Parties

For companies, convertible notes provide a quick and flexible way to raise capital without undergoing a lengthy valuation process. For investors, the potential upside lies in the conversion to equity at favorable terms. However, both parties must carefully negotiate the notes' terms to ensure fair treatment, especially in regard to the discount rate, valuation cap, and interest rate.

Convertible note agreements typically include the following:

- Loan amount
- Interest rate
- Conversion discount
- Valuation cap
- Maturity date

The terms may also specify what happens if the note matures before a conversion event, such as requiring repayment or automatic conversion to equity.

Warrants

Overview of Warrant Agreements

Warrants are financial instruments that give the holder the right but not the obligation to purchase a company's stock at a predetermined price known as the exercise price within a specific time frame. Warrants are often issued alongside other securities, such as debt to sweeten the deal for investors.

Exercise Price and Expiration Date

The exercise price or strike price is the price at which the warrant holder can purchase shares of the company. This price is usually set higher than the current market price to incentivize the warrant holder to invest more in the company's future growth. Warrants also have an expiration date after which the holder loses the right to purchase the stock.

Potential Benefits and Risks for Investors and Issuers

For investors, warrants offer the potential for significant gains if the company's stock price increases above the exercise price. For companies, issuing warrants can help attract investors without immediately diluting ownership. However, if too many warrants are exercised at once, it can lead to significant dilution for existing shareholders.

Warrant agreements typically include the following:

- The number of shares that can be purchased
- Exercise price
- Expiration date

- Any vesting schedules or conditions under which the warrants can be exercised

Simple Agreement for Future Equity

Introduction to a Simple Agreement for Future Equity

A simple agreement for future equity (SAFE) is a relatively new financial instrument used to raise capital from investors without selling equity up front. Unlike convertible notes, SAFEs do not accrue interest or have a maturity date. Instead, they convert into equity at the time of a future financing round typically at a discounted valuation or with a valuation cap.

Key Terms and Differences from Traditional Securities

SAFEs are simpler and more flexible than convertible notes, making them popular in early-stage fundraising. They do not require repayment, and the conversion mechanics are typically more straightforward. However, unlike convertible notes, SAFEs offer no recourse for investors if the company fails to raise another round of financing.

Pros and Cons in Early-Stage Fundraising

The primary advantage of SAFEs is their simplicity and speed, allowing companies to raise funds quickly without complex debt or equity negotiations. However, because they lack a maturity date, investors assume more risk because there is no guarantee of conversion or repayment.

SAFE agreements include key terms like the following:

- Valuation cap
- Discount rate
- The trigger for conversion into equity

Some SAFEs also include "most-favored-nation" clauses, ensuring that early investors receive the same terms as later ones.

Limited Liability Company Membership Interests

Definition and Characteristics of Membership Interests in Limited Liability Companies

In a limited liability company (LLC), investors typically receive membership interests that represent ownership stakes in the company. These interests entitle holders to a share of the profits and losses as well as participation in the management of the company depending on the terms of the operating agreement.

Ownership Rights and Distributions

Members of an LLC are typically entitled to distributions based on their ownership percentage. However, unlike shareholders in a corporation, LLC members may also participate in the management of the business unless the company is structured as a manager-managed LLC.

Management Participation and Control Dynamics

LLC membership interests may come with voting rights that allow members to influence major business decisions. The operating agreement often dictates how much control each member has and under what circumstances decisions can be made without unanimous consent.

Deal terms for LLC membership interests often include the following:

- Percentage of ownership
- Voting rights
- Distribution rights
- Buyout provisions in case a member wishes to exit the company

Investment Contracts

Overview of Investment Contracts

Investment contracts are "hybrid" contractual arrangements in which investors provide capital in exchange for a contractual right to a return on investment based on the company's performance. These contracts often do not confer ownership but instead establish a financial obligation. However, some contracts may also grant equity (or the right to convert to equity) based upon some metric. In practice, the possibilities are essentially endless in how an investment contract can be structured.

Terms and Conditions for Investment and Returns

The terms of investment contracts typically include the amount of capital provided, the rate of return, and the conditions under which the investor will be repaid. For example, an investment contract may stipulate that the company must repay the principal amount plus interest by a certain date or share a percentage of gross sales, revenue, or net profits with an investor.

Considerations for Investors and Issuers

For investors, investment contracts provide a clearer path to repayment, often with less risk than equity investments. For issuers, these contracts can raise capital without giving up ownership, but they come with the obligation to repay funds or pay a sizable share of revenue which may strain cash flow.

Investment contracts often include terms such as the following:

- Investment amount
- Interest rate or profit sharing arrangement
- Payment schedule
- Conditions of repayment

Rights to collateral securing the investment may also sometimes be offered or negotiated.

Limited Partnerships

Explanation of Limited Partnership Structures

A limited partnership (LP) consists of at least one general partner who manages the business and one or more limited partners who provide capital but do not participate in day-to-day operations. Limited partners have limited liability, meaning their risk is confined to the amount of their investment.

General Partners and Limited Partners' Roles and Responsibilities

The general partner is responsible for managing the partnership and is personally liable for its obligations. Limited partners are passive investors who benefit from the partnership's profits but are not involved in management decisions.

Profit Sharing and Liability Implications

Profits in an LP are typically shared according to the LP agreement. LPs are shielded from liabilities beyond their initial investment, making this structure attractive for investors seeking minimal involvement and limited risk.

Deal terms for LPs include the following:

- Percentage of ownership
- Profit-sharing arrangements
- Conditions under which the partnership may be dissolved (e.g., general partner may be replaced, consent of the limited partners may be required)

* * * * *

As you can see, understanding the various types of securities and deal terms is crucial for structuring a successful capital raise. Whether you're issuing common stock or preferred shares or using more complex instruments like convertible notes or warrants, each option carries its own set of advantages and considerations for both the issuer and the investor. By carefully selecting the right type of security and negotiating fair deal terms, you can align your capital-raising efforts with your long-term business goals, ensuring both flexibility and protection as your company grows.

CHAPTER **4**

Investor Types and Where to Find Them

If you've ever gone fishing (or thought about fishing), you intuitively know that where you fish and what kind of bait you use is crucial to say nothing about timing. For example, searching for large game fish such as marlin or mahi-mahi in your local freshwater pond would be a bad idea. Likewise, trout and salmon are only to be found in mountain lakes and swiftly flowing rivers, not in the ocean, and will only go for certain kinds of bait during particular seasons or times of day. And if you go whale hunting, be prepared to travel far, be patient, and spend considerable resources to reel them into the boat (presuming you can find one in the first place).

Investors are no different.

Raising capital involves understanding the different types of investors and knowing where to find them. Each investor category has its own preferences, risk tolerance, and expectations, so tailoring your approach to the right type of investor is crucial. In this chapter, we'll explore the major types of investors and the best strategies to connect with them.

Investor Types

Angel Investors

Definition and Characteristics

Angel investors are typically high-net-worth individuals who invest their personal capital in early-stage companies. They often have entrepreneurial backgrounds and are willing to take on higher risks in exchange for the potential of significant returns. Unlike institutional investors, angel investors usually make smaller investments and may take a more personal interest in the businesses they support.

Investment Preferences and Criteria

Angel investors tend to look for companies with strong growth potential, a compelling product or service, and a capable management team. They are often more flexible than VCs in terms of deal structure and valuation, but they expect a significant equity stake in return for their investment. Many angel investors focus on specific industries where they have the expertise that allows them to offer valuable guidance in addition to capital.

Benefits of Attracting Angel Investors

One of the major benefits of attracting angel investors is the speed at which they can make decisions. Unlike larger institutional investors, angels are often less encumbered by bureaucratic processes allowing for quicker access to capital. Additionally, angel investors often bring their networks and experience to the table providing more than just financial backing. This can be a huge advantage for entrepreneurs looking to grow their businesses rapidly.

Venture Capitalists

Definition and Role in the Investment Landscape

VCs are professional investors who manage funds pooled from various sources, including institutional investors and high-net-worth individuals. VCs typically invest in high-growth companies focusing on sectors like technology, health care, and fintech. They seek to make large returns on their investments by taking equity positions in companies they believe have the potential to scale significantly.

Differences Between Early-Stage and Later-Stage VCs

There are important distinctions between early-stage and later-stage VCs. Early-stage VCs focus on companies that are just starting out often providing seed funding to help them grow from concept to product. They usually take on higher risk, but in return, they seek larger equity stakes. Later-stage VCs invest in more mature companies that have established products, customers, and revenue streams. These investors look for businesses that are scaling rapidly and are often close to an exit event such as an IPO or acquisition.

Investment Process and Expectations of VCs

The VC investment process is rigorous and often involves multiple rounds of due diligence, financial analysis, and meetings with the company's management team. VCs expect rapid growth and are heavily focused on metrics such as market size, customer acquisition, and scalability. Entrepreneurs should be prepared to articulate a clear path to growth and exit when pitching to VCs. In return, VCs provide not only capital but also strategic advice, industry connections, and help with scaling the business.

Institutional Investors

Definition and Types

Institutional investors include large organizations such as pension funds, endowments, insurance companies, and mutual funds. These investors manage vast pools of capital and tend to focus on more mature companies or investment vehicles such as private equity funds or VC funds rather than direct investments in start-ups.

Investment Decision Criteria

Institutional investors often have strict criteria for making investment decisions focusing on factors like track record, risk management, and regulatory compliance. They require thorough due diligence and are particularly concerned with governance and stability. While they may not invest directly in early-stage companies, institutional investors are key players in later-stage funding rounds or as limited partners in VC or private equity funds.

Importance of Building Relationships with Institutional Investors

Building relationships with institutional investors can open doors to substantial funding down the line. Institutional investors may not invest directly in your start-up, but if you're working with a venture fund backed by an institution, that connection can provide stability and confidence for future investors. Establishing credibility early on and building a track record will make it easier to attract institutional capital as your business grows.

Family Offices

Definition and Characteristics

Family offices manage the wealth of high-net-worth families and are becoming increasingly important players in the private capital markets. These offices manage a range of investments, including direct investments in private companies, real estate, and alternative assets. Family offices tend to have a long-term investment horizon and are often more flexible in their approach compared to institutional investors.

Considerations When Approaching Family Offices

Family offices can vary greatly in their investment strategies and decision-making processes because they are often influenced by the preferences and goals of the family they represent. Some focus on preserving wealth through conservative investments, whereas others are willing to take on more risk for higher returns. When approaching a family office, it's essential to understand their objectives and tailor your pitch accordingly.

Benefits of Securing Investments from Family Offices

One of the primary benefits of family offices is their flexibility. Unlike VC funds or institutional investors, family offices are not bound by strict mandates allowing them to structure deals creatively. They also tend to take a long-term view, making them ideal partners for companies with longer paths to profitability. Additionally, family offices often provide patient capital, meaning they are willing to invest without the immediate pressure of exit.

Accredited Investors

Definition and Regulatory Requirements

Accredited investors are individuals or entities that meet specific financial criteria set by the SEC. To qualify, an individual must have a net worth of at least $1 million (excluding their primary residence) or an annual income exceeding $200,000 (or $300,000 with a spouse). Accredited investors are deemed financially sophisticated and able to bear the risks of private investments.

Tapping into the Network of Accredited Investors

Accredited investors can be a valuable source of capital, especially for early-stage companies. Entrepreneurs can tap into networks of accredited investors through angel groups, online platforms, and professional networks. These investors often seek high-risk, high-reward opportunities and are more willing to invest in early-stage ventures than institutional investors.

Leveraging Accredited Investor Platforms and Networks

Several platforms cater specifically to accredited investors, connecting them with start-ups seeking capital. Platforms like AngelList, SeedInvest, and Fundable allow entrepreneurs to reach a broader audience of accredited investors. These platforms streamline the investment process by providing due diligence, legal documentation, and escrow services.

Non-accredited Investors

Definition and Considerations for Engaging with Non-accredited Investors

Non-accredited investors do not meet the SEC's financial criteria for accredited investors, meaning they have fewer resources to conduct their own due diligence making delivery of a full-disclosure PPM to such investors critical. "Friends and family" typically fall into this category, who often play a pivotal role in providing "pre-seed" or "pre-launch" funding to help get a new venture off the ground. Engaging with non-accredited investors requires adherence to strict regulatory frameworks, such as the SEC's Reg CF, Rule 506(b) under Regulation D, or Regulation A or federal and state statutory exemptions such as Section 4(a)(2) of the Securities Act and applicable state limited offering exemptions, to ensure compliance.

Using Crowdfunding Platforms and Regulations

Crowdfunding platforms like Kickstarter, WeFunder, and Republic have made it easier for entrepreneurs to raise capital from non-accredited investors. Under Reg CF, start-ups can raise up to $5 million in a 12-month period from the general public. These platforms provide a unique opportunity to raise smaller amounts of capital from a large pool of investors, but they also require full compliance with regulatory requirements including disclosure of financials and business risks through a comprehensive offering statement (similar to a PPM) and a Form C filing with the SEC.

Strategies for Finding Investors

Networking and Relationship Building

Building a Strong Professional Network

Networking remains one of the most effective ways to connect with investors. Building a strong professional network involves not only attending events but also forming genuine relationships with potential investors, advisors, and peers. Entrepreneurs should make a point to stay active in their industry's ecosystem by nurturing relationships with investors over time.

Attending Industry Events and Conferences

Industry events and conferences are ideal places to meet potential investors. Many events feature networking sessions, panel discussions, and presentations that allow entrepreneurs to interact with investors in an informal setting. Being prepared with a concise elevator pitch and a compelling story will increase your chances of capturing investor interest.

Using Personal Connections and Introductions

Leveraging personal connections is another effective way to find investors. A warm introduction from a mutual contact can open doors and increase the likelihood of securing a meeting. Entrepreneurs should not hesitate to ask for referrals from friends, colleagues, and mentors who may have connections with investors.

Online Platforms and Networks

Popular Platforms for Connecting with Investors

Online platforms like AngelList, Gust, and SeedInvest have revolutionized the way entrepreneurs connect with investors. These platforms allow start-ups to create profiles, share information about their businesses, and raise capital from accredited investors. The platforms streamline the fundraising process, making it easier to manage investor outreach and due diligence.

Leveraging Social Media and Online Communities

Social media can be a powerful tool for attracting investors. Platforms like LinkedIn, Twitter, and even niche communities such as Reddit can help entrepreneurs build their brand, share updates, and engage with potential investors. Regularly posting relevant content and actively participating in discussions can increase visibility and establish credibility in your industry.

Maximizing Visibility and Reach of Investment Opportunities

Maximizing the visibility of your investment opportunity involves using all available channels to reach a broader audience. This can include participating in pitch competitions, partnering with accelerators, and using email marketing to keep potential investors informed of your progress.

Professional Service Providers

Engaging with Professionals (Investment Bankers, Attorneys, Consultants)

Professional service providers such as investment bankers, attorneys, and consultants can be valuable partners in the capital-raising process. These professionals often have relationships with investors and can facilitate introductions. Additionally, they can help structure deals, ensure regulatory compliance, and provide strategic advice.

* * * * *

As we've explored, identifying the right types of investors and knowing where to find them is essential to raising capital effectively. Whether you're targeting angel investors, VCs, or institutional investors, each group comes with its own expectations, risk tolerance, and investment criteria. By understanding these dynamics and tailoring your approach, you can attract the ideal investors who both provide funding and offer strategic value to your business. In the end, building strong, lasting relationships with investors is just as important as securing the capital itself.

CHAPTER **5**

Essential Elements of a Private Placement Memorandum

Your PPM is the most important document in your private offering. It is the "selling document" in every legal sense of the word.

If you contact a Financial Industry Regulatory Authority (FINRA) broker–dealer to help you find investors, the first thing they will ask for is your PPM.

If the SEC or a state securities regulator ever knocks on your door, the first thing they will demand to see is your PPM.

Your PPM enables you to satisfy US federal and state anti-fraud securities laws (i.e., your "Get out of jail free" card) and is your "shield" and primary defense tool (i.e., your "dismiss this lawsuit" card) in the event investors ever turn against you.

Your PPM (or in the context of Reg CF, your offering statement) serves as your comprehensive disclosure document that informs potential investors about the terms of the investment, the company's business, and the associated risks. For entrepreneurs raising capital, the PPM is a critical tool in ensuring transparency and regulatory compliance.

Your PPM enables you to satisfy US federal and state anti-fraud securities laws (i.e., your "Get out of jail free" card) and is your "shield" and primary defense tool (i.e., your "dismiss this lawsuit" card) in the event investors turn against you.

In this chapter, we will cover the essential elements of a PPM detailing its purpose, structure, and the key sections that should be included.

Purpose and Structure of a PPM

Understanding the Purpose of a PPM in a Private Offering

The primary purpose of a PPM is to provide full and fair disclosure to potential investors. It outlines the terms of the offering, the business's operations, and the risks involved helping investors make informed decisions. The PPM also plays a vital role in complying with securities laws, particularly Regulation D and other federal and state requirements ensuring that the offering qualifies for private placement exemptions.

Key Components and Sections of a Typical PPM

A well-structured PPM includes several key sections each designed to present specific information about the investment. These sections typically include an executive summary, a detailed company overview, the terms of the securities offering, risk factors, management team bios, financial information, and legal considerations. The PPM is often supplemented by appendices or exhibits containing subscription agreements, financial statements, and any other "material" or relevant documents.

Importance of Clear and Concise Language in Conveying Information

One of the challenges of drafting a PPM is striking the right balance between legal thoroughness and readability. While the document must be comprehensive and legally sound, it's also important to present information in a way that is clear and engaging for investors. Overly technical language or unnecessary legal jargon can deter potential investors, so clarity should be a top priority.

Executive Summary

Role and Significance of the Executive Summary

The executive summary is arguably the most critical part of the PPM because it's the first section potential investors will read after receiving it. It needs to quickly capture their attention and give them a clear understanding of the opportunity at hand. The executive summary should provide a concise overview of the company, the business model, and the key terms of the investment. It also should be consistent with any other ancillary selling literature or marketing materials (e.g., your pitch deck, website, financial forecast, etc.) you may be using, all of which should have prominent disclaimers redirecting the investor's attention back to the PPM.

Highlighting Key Investment Highlights and Terms

This section should highlight the most attractive elements of the investment, such as the company's unique value proposition, its growth potential, and any competitive advantages it holds. Additionally, the executive summary should summarize the key

> *Marketing materials (e.g., your pitch deck, website, financial forecast) ... should have prominent disclaimers redirecting the investor's attention back to the PPM.*

terms of the offering including the type of securities being offered, the amount of capital being raised, and the intended use of proceeds.

Capturing Investor Attention and Generating Interest

The goal of the executive summary is to generate enough interest to encourage investors to continue reading the PPM. It should be concise yet compelling to make a strong case for why the investment is worth their time and money. Entrepreneurs should focus on delivering a clear, persuasive narrative that aligns with the expectations and interests of their target investors.

Company Overview and Business Plan

Presenting a Comprehensive Overview of the Company

The company overview provides investors with a detailed look at the business including its history, mission, and operations. This section should also include information on the company's core products or services, its market positioning, and any notable achievements to date. The goal is to give investors a deep understanding of what the company does and how it generates revenue.

Describing the Business Model, Industry Analysis, and Competitive Landscape

An effective PPM includes an analysis of the company's business model, explaining how it plans to generate and grow revenue. Entrepreneurs should also provide an analysis of the industry in which the company operates, highlighting key trends, market opportunities, and potential threats. Finally, the competitive landscape should be addressed outlining the company's position relative to its competitors and explaining how it plans to differentiate itself.

Outlining the Growth Strategy and Future Potential

Investors want to know how a company plans to grow and scale. The PPM should include a clear growth strategy outlining both short-term goals and long-term objectives. This might include product development plans, market expansion strategies, and key partnerships. Showing investors how the company intends to achieve sustainable growth is crucial to securing their interest.

Investment Terms and Securities Offering

Detailing the Terms and Conditions of the Investment Opportunity

This section of the PPM should clearly outline the terms of the securities offering. It includes details on the type of securities being offered (e.g., equity, preferred stock, convertible debt), the price per share or unit, and the total amount being raised. Additionally, the document should specify the intended use of the capital, providing transparency around how the funds will be allocated.

Describing the Securities Being Offered (e.g., Equity, Debt, Preferred Shares)

Depending on the type of security being offered, the PPM should include a detailed description of its features and terms. For example, if the offering involves preferred stock, the PPM should explain the dividend rights, liquidation preferences, and any conversion or redemption features. If convertible notes are being offered, the document should describe the conversion mechanics and any triggers for conversion into equity.

Investors will want to understand what rights and privileges they will have as part of the offering. This section should detail any voting rights, board representation, or anti-dilution protections that come with the securities. Additionally, it's important to disclose any restrictions on the transfer or sale of the securities as well as any lock-up periods.

Risk Factors and Disclosures

Identifying and Disclosing Potential Risks Associated with the Investment

The risk factors section is a critical part of the PPM because it provides full disclosure of the risks that could affect the investment. This may include market risks, regulatory risks, competitive risks, and financial risks. Transparency is key here; failing to disclose a material risk could lead to legal liabilities for the company and its management.

Providing Comprehensive Risk Factors and Risk Mitigation Strategies

In addition to identifying risks, the PPM should discuss any strategies the company has in place to mitigate those risks. For example, if the company operates in a highly competitive industry, it might outline its plans for maintaining a competitive edge. If regulatory risks are a concern, the PPM should describe the company's compliance procedures and legal safeguards.

Ensuring Compliance with Securities Regulations and Legal Requirements

It's crucial to ensure that the PPM complies with all relevant securities regulations including those set forth by the SEC and applicable state blue sky laws. The risk factors section should also address any legal considerations related to the offering such as potential litigation or regulatory changes that could impact the company.

Management Team and Key Personnel

Introducing the Management Team and Their Qualifications

The management team plays a significant role in an investor's decision-making process. The PPM should introduce the key members of the management team providing a brief biography for each individual. This should highlight their relevant experience, qualifications, and track record of success.

Highlighting the Expertise and Experience of Key Personnel

Investors want to see that the company is led by a capable, experienced team. In this section, entrepreneurs should emphasize the expertise of their team, particularly in areas that are critical to the success of the business. This could include previous entrepreneurial ventures, industry-specific knowledge, or experience in scaling companies.

Demonstrating the Team's Ability to Execute the Business Plan

It's not enough to have a compelling business plan; investors need to feel confident that the team can execute it. The PPM should make a strong case for why the management team is well-positioned to achieve the company's growth objectives, highlighting any past successes and relevant skills.

Financial Information

Presenting Current Financial Statements

If the company has been operating for some time, the PPM should include current and up-to-date financial statements, such as income disclosures, balance sheets, and cash flow statements. These documents provide investors with insight into the company's current financial health and performance to date. Of course, if the company is brand new, your financial statements will be "zeroes" or show minimum assets. Don't worry about this too much because investors will be focused more on what they believe might be your company's future potential not its current liquidation value. Don't make the mistake of inserting *pro forma* financial statements in the place of your current, actual numbers as investors may be unintentionally misled otherwise.

Including Disclosure of Any Material Events or Financial Risks

If there are any material events that could affect the company's financial position such as significant liabilities, pending lawsuits, or changes in leadership, these should be disclosed in the PPM. Transparency is key in building trust with investors, and full disclosure of any financial risks is necessary for compliance with securities laws.

What About Financial Forecasts and Pro Forma?

Many investors are also interested in seeing financial forecasts that project the company's future performance. You'll also want to paint a picture of what you believe is realistically possible for the future at this stage in the life of your company. However, bear in mind that like weather forecasts, even the most sophisticated financial forecasts are invariably wrong! Rarely do companies ever "hit their numbers" with precision. And because the PPM is the "selling document" (i.e., the document investors will legally rely upon in making an investment decision), you don't to want to have a financial forecast used as a cudgel against you by investors in the future (always with "20/20" hindsight, of course) in case things don't pan out as well as you initially imagined.

So, in practice, our clients have found it's best to only use a financial forecast as a stand-alone document or as part of a pitch deck or other selling literature outside of the PPM with a disclaimer, of course, cautioning the investor not to rely upon it and encouraging them to read the PPM. In any event, *pro forma* financials or financial forecasts should be realistic and based on sound assumptions. Entrepreneurs would do well to be cautious about making overly optimistic projections because unrealistic expectations or "pie-in-the-sky" numbers can erode investor confidence.

Like weather forecasts, even the most sophisticated financial forecasts are invariably wrong!

Only use a financial forecast as a stand-alone document or as part of a pitch deck or other selling literature outside of the PPM with a disclaimer.

Legal Considerations

"Bad Actor" Exclusions

Certain securities regulations often include provisions known as "bad actor" exclusions, which disqualify certain individuals from participating in private offerings if they have a history of securities violations or other misconduct. When preparing a PPM, consult with your securities attorney regarding whether any members of the management team or key personnel fall under these exclusions.

Conflicts of Interest

Any potential conflicts of interest such as relationships between the management team and investors or third-party service providers should be disclosed in the PPM. This transparency is crucial for maintaining investor trust and ensuring compliance with securities laws.

Material Legal Proceedings, Past and Present

The PPM should also disclose any material legal proceedings involving the company or its key personnel. This includes past lawsuits, regulatory actions, or any ongoing litigation that could impact the company's operations or financial health.

Subscription Process and Legal Considerations

Outlining the Subscription Process and Investor Eligibility Requirements

The final section of the PPM should outline the process for investors to subscribe to the offering. This includes the documentation they will need to complete (e.g., a suitability questionnaire, subscription agreement), the timeline for submitting their investment, and any eligibility requirements they must meet (e.g., verification of their accredited investor status).

Compliance with Securities Laws and Regulations (Regulation D, Blue Sky Laws, etc.)

Finally, the PPM should ensure that the offering complies with all relevant securities laws including Regulation D (for private offerings) and any applicable state "blue sky" laws. This section should also describe any notice or filing requirements or other regulatory obligations the company will need to fulfill in connection with the offering.

*   *   *   *   *

As we've discussed, your PPM is an essential document in any private offering providing potential investors with the comprehensive information they need to make informed decisions. From the executive summary to the detailed risk factors, every section of the PPM plays a critical role in establishing transparency, trust, and compliance with securities regulations.

Given the complexity and legal intricacies involved, attempting to write a PPM on your own can lead to costly mistakes.

Given the complexity and legal intricacies involved, attempting to write a PPM on your own can lead to costly mistakes. It is highly recommended that you engage competent and seasoned securities counsel or a law firm experienced in preparing PPMs. Doing so will not only ensure that your offering is compliant with all relevant regulations but also give investors the confidence that your business is professionally managed and legally sound.

CHAPTER **6**

PPM Disclosures: What Is Required?

As we discussed in the prior chapter, a Private Placement Memorandum (PPM) is a critical document in any private securities offerings. Its most important function is to provide potential investors with all material information relevant to the investment. This chapter will explore the concept of material information, what types of disclosures are required in a PPM, and the potential legal consequences of failing to disclose material information properly.

Importance of Material Information and Disclosures in Securities Offerings

At the core of any securities offering is the principle that investors must be provided with all material information they need to make an informed decision. "Material information" is any detail that a reasonable investor would consider important when deciding whether to invest. Failing to disclose such information can result in significant legal and regulatory consequences for the issuer.

Overview of Securities Laws and Regulations Governing Materiality

Several securities laws govern the requirement to disclose material information including the Securities Act of 1933, which lays the foundation for public and private offerings in the US. Under Regulation D, which governs private placements. Issuers are not subject to the same extensive disclosure requirements as public companies, but they are still required to provide material information to accredited investors to prevent fraud and misrepresentation. The SEC can take action against issuers who make material omissions or misstatements in their PPMs, so compliance is paramount.

Understanding Material Information

What Is Material Information?

"Material information" refers to any fact that would influence an investor's decision to buy or sell a security. The definition of "materiality" is broad and can encompass a wide range of facts about the company its operations, financial condition, legal status, or even external factors such as regulatory changes or market conditions.

The Supreme Court has held that a fact is material if there is "a substantial likelihood that the ... fact would have been viewed by the reasonable investor as having significantly altered the 'total mix' of information made available" *TSC Industries v. Northway, Inc.*, 426 US 438, 449 (1976); *Basic, Inc. v. Levinson*, 485 US 224 (1988).

Note: Keep in mind the phrase "would have been viewed." Courts always have the benefit of 20/20 hindsight, which doesn't always cut in your favor.

Criteria for Determining Materiality

Determining whether information is material requires judgment, but several factors help guide this assessment. These include the size and significance of the information in relation to the company's overall operations, its potential impact on the company's financial position or business strategy, and whether it could affect the company's competitive standing or risk profile.

Key Factors Influencing Materiality Assessments

Several factors can influence whether information is considered material. These include the company's stage of development (Early-stage companies may have different material risks than mature firms.), the industry it operates

A fact is "material" if there is a substantial likelihood that the ... fact would have been viewed by the reasonable investor as having significantly altered the "total mix" of information made available."

in (industry-specific risks such as regulatory changes), and the nature of the investment (e.g., equity vs. debt). Issuers should be conservative in their approach and disclose information if there is any doubt about its materiality.

Material Disclosures in Securities Offerings

Types of Information Typically Considered Material

Certain types of information are almost always considered material in securities offerings. These include the following:

- Financial performance data
- Key risks facing the business
- Significant contracts
- Information about the company's management team

Disclosing this information allows investors to assess the company's health and potential for growth as well as any risks they may face.

Financial Information and Performance

One of the most critical types of material information is the company's financial performance. This includes historical financial statements, details of any debt obligations, and estimates of future revenue and earnings potential. Investors use this information to evaluate the company's financial health, profitability, and likelihood of generating a return on their investment.

Business Operations and Strategies

Investors also need a clear understanding of how the company operates and its strategies for growth. This includes information on the company's products or services, target markets, competitive landscape, and overall business model. Any significant changes in the company's operations or strategies should also be disclosed.

Risk Factors and Uncertainties

All investments come with risk, and it is essential to disclose any material risks that could affect the company's ability to achieve its objectives. This could include market risks, regulatory risks, operational risks, and financial risks. Providing a thorough list of risk factors gives investors a clearer picture of the challenges the company may face and helps protect the issuer from legal liabilities.

Legal and Regulatory Matters

Material legal and regulatory matters should be disclosed, including any past, present, and potential lawsuits or regulatory actions against the company and its principals as well as potential compliance issues. Investors need to understand any legal risks that could affect the company's operations or financial condition.

Management and Key Personnel

The management team plays a critical role in the success of any business, and their qualifications, experience, and track record should be fully disclosed in the PPM. If any key personnel are involved in prior misconduct or litigation or if there are significant changes to the leadership team, these should be disclosed as well.

Material Contracts and Agreements

Any significant contracts such as supplier agreements, licensing deals, or partnership arrangements should be disclosed. These contracts could have a substantial impact on the company's future performance, and their terms should be clear to investors.

Litigation and Disputes

Investors should be made aware of any ongoing or potential litigation that could affect the company. Even if the company believes it will prevail in a legal dispute, it is essential to disclose the nature of the litigation, the risks involved, and any potential financial liabilities.

Industry-Specific Considerations

Depending on the industry, certain disclosures may be more material than others. For example, a biotechnology company may need to disclose the status of clinical trials and regulatory approvals, whereas a financial services firm might need to disclose details about regulatory capital requirements or cybersecurity risks.

Consequences of Inadequate Disclosure

Legal Implications of Material Misstatements or Omissions

Failing to disclose material information or providing misleading information can have serious legal consequences. Under US securities laws, issuers are liable for material misstatements or omissions that mislead investors. The company's officers and directors may also face personal liability if they fail to meet their disclosure obligations.

Civil Liabilities and Investor Remedies

Investors who suffer losses due to inadequate disclosures may have legal recourse against the issuer. Civil liabilities can include rescission rights, which allow investors to void their purchase of securities or claims for damages based on fraud or negligence. These claims can result in costly settlements or judgments against the company.

Regulatory Enforcement Actions

The SEC has the authority to bring civil enforcement actions against companies that fail to comply with disclosure requirements. These actions can result in fines, penalties, and other sanctions, including the suspension or prohibition of future offerings. In addition (and arguably more concerning), state securities regulators can bring not only civil enforcement actions under their own state securities laws but also the pursuit of criminal prosecution against issuers and promoters they deem fraudulent or who they believe are endangering investors in their state.

As you can see, ensuring that all material information is properly disclosed is crucial to avoiding regulatory scrutiny.

Best Practices for Material Disclosures

Importance of Thorough Due Diligence

Issuers should work with their securities counsel and conduct thorough internal due diligence to ensure that all information conveyed and disclosed in their PPM is materially correct. This process includes reviewing the company's financials, legal matters, contracts, and operations to identify any potential risks or liabilities that need to be disclosed. Engaging in a comprehensive due diligence process reduces the risk of omissions and strengthens the overall quality of the disclosure.

Engaging Legal and Compliance Professionals

Working with experienced legal and compliance professionals is essential in drafting a PPM that meets regulatory requirements. These experts can help identify material information; ensure compliance with securities laws; and draft clear, concise language that mitigates the risk of litigation.

> *PPMs often quickly get "stale," especially if you pivot or market conditions change and need to be refreshed ... We typically recommend a review of your PPM with securities counsel at least once every six months to make sure everything being disclosed continues to be materially correct.*

Periodic Updates and Amendments

Material disclosures are not a one-time requirement. PPMs often quickly get "stale," especially if you pivot or market conditions change and need to be refreshed. If circumstances change after the PPM has been issued such as new financial data or significant business developments, the company may need to issue amendments or updates to keep investors informed. We typically recommend a review of your PPM with securities counsel at least once every six months to make sure everything being disclosed continues to be materially correct. Failure to provide timely updates can lead to legal risks even after the initial offering has closed.

Maintaining Accurate and Up-to-Date Records

Maintaining accurate records is a key component of effective disclosure. Companies should have systems in place to track material developments, such as changes in financial performance, legal matters, or business strategy, and ensure that this information is readily available for disclosure in the PPM or any subsequent updates.

*　*　*　*　*

In conclusion, providing clear, accurate, and comprehensive disclosures is not just a best practice, it's a legal obligation under securities law. Failing to meet these standards can lead to severe consequences for your business and its leadership.

For example, in 2024, the SEC charged Ideanomics, Inc., with fraudulent activities for misleading the public about the company's financial performance. Ideanomics, along with several executives, overstated revenues by more than $40 million and used deceptive tactics to avoid disclosing losses. As a result, the company faced significant financial penalties, and several key executives were barred from serving in leadership positions for years (see *sec.gov/newsroom/press-releases/2024-94*).

This case serves as a powerful reminder that inadequate or inaccurate disclosures can damage not only your reputation but also your company's future. To protect your business and ensure compliance, it is essential to work closely with seasoned securities counsel when preparing disclosure documents. Proper legal guidance will help you avoid costly mistakes and safeguard your investors' trust.

CHAPTER **7**

Subscription Documents and Closing Investor Subscriptions

The final stage in the capital-raising process involves closing investor subscriptions, a critical step that solidifies the legal and financial relationship between the company and its investors. This chapter will guide entrepreneurs through the practical considerations of closing investor subscriptions, understanding subscription documents, and ensuring compliance with investor suitability requirements.

Practical Considerations When Closing an Investor

Closing an investor subscription involves more than just signing paperwork. Entrepreneurs must ensure that the process is smooth, efficient, and transparent for the investor. It is essential to provide clear, concise instructions and ensure that all required documentation is complete and compliant with regulatory requirements. Putting yourself in the investor's shoes during this process can help you anticipate and resolve potential concerns ensuring a positive experience for the investor and building trust.

DocuSign, AdobeSign, and PDFs

In today's digital age, most subscription documents are handled electronically through platforms like DocuSign or AdobeSign. These platforms allow both the company and investors to execute documents securely and efficiently. PDFs are the standard format for these documents because they maintain the integrity of the original content and are widely accepted. When using these tools, make sure the process is seamless for investors and provide clear guidance on how to complete and submit the forms electronically.

Putting Yourself in the Investor's Shoes

To close an investor subscription successfully, it's crucial to understand the process from the investor's perspective. Investors are likely to have questions about the documents they are signing, the security of their personal information, and the timeline for finalizing the investment. By proactively addressing these concerns and offering clear communication, you can reduce friction and ensure the closing process goes smoothly.

Instruction Page

Keep It Simple!

The instruction page for closing an investor subscription should be simple and straightforward. Avoid overloading investors with technical jargon or unnecessary details. A clean, easy-to-follow instruction page enhances the investor's experience and reduces the likelihood of errors or delays in the subscription process.

Checklist

Providing a checklist helps investors know exactly what is required of them. The checklist should include items such as completed suitability questionnaires, signed subscription agreements, and bank wire instructions. A clear checklist can significantly reduce the back-and-forth communication that often arises when documents are incomplete or missing.

Clear Instructions

Each step in the subscription process should come with clear, concise instructions. This includes guidance on filling out forms, verifying investor status, and submitting documents electronically. Be sure to specify deadlines for document submission and any other time-sensitive information. Clarity is essential to avoid confusion and ensure that the closing process moves forward without unnecessary delays.

Bank Wire Information

Accurate bank wire information is critical to avoid any miscommunication or errors in the transfer of funds. Make sure to provide detailed instructions for wiring funds, including the correct bank account number, routing information, and any specific reference details. It's also a good practice to include contact information for someone who can assist investors with any questions or issues related to the transfer process.

Suitability Questionnaire

Key Subscriber Information

The suitability questionnaire collects essential information about the subscriber, including the following:

- Name
- Address
- Email address
- Telephone number
- State or jurisdiction of residency
- Taxpayer identification number

This information is both necessary for legal and regulatory purposes and ensures that the company has accurate records of each investor. These data play a critical role in maintaining communication and managing relationships with investors.

Subscriber Suitability

One of the primary functions of the suitability questionnaire is to determine whether the subscriber qualifies as an accredited or non-accredited investor. For accredited investors, specific criteria must be met, including income or net worth thresholds set by the SEC. Non-accredited investors are subject to additional requirements under securities laws, particularly in offerings that rely on Regulation D exemptions, such as demonstrating that they are sophisticated enough to understand the merits and risks of investing or that they are represented by such a person.

Subscribers must also indicate the entity through which they are investing such as a natural person, corporation, partnership, LLC, family trust, or self-directed IRA. Each entity type may have different tax and legal implications, so it is important to collect accurate information at this stage.

Subscriber Representation(s)

Subscribers must make certain representations about their status as accredited or non-accredited investors. Under certain securities law exemptions, such as Rule 506(b) of Regulation D, investors may self-certify their status. However, verification of accredited investor status is required under Rule 506(c) of Regulation D where general solicitation is permitted.

Verification of Accredited Investors

There are several ways to verify accredited investor status, including the following:

- Review of tax returns or financial statements
- Third-party verification by attorneys, accountants, or broker–dealers

When Is Self-Verification Allowed?

Self-verification may be permitted in offerings where the issuer has a preexisting relationship with the investor and where the offering does not involve general solicitation. In these cases, investors may simply attest to their accredited status without providing supporting documentation.

Non-accredited Investor Suitability

For non-accredited investors, the suitability questionnaire must assess their financial sophistication and ability to bear the risks of the investment. This may include evaluating their income, net worth, and investment experience. Non-accredited investors are typically limited in the amount they can invest, and issuers must take extra care to ensure they are suitable for the offering.

Subscriber Signature(s)

At the conclusion of the suitability questionnaire, the subscriber must sign to affirm the accuracy of the information provided and their understanding of the representations they are making. This signature is essential for both regulatory compliance and legal protections for the issuer.

The Subscription Agreement

Key Elements

The subscription agreement is a legally binding contract between the investor and the company. It outlines the terms and conditions of the investor's participation in the offering, including the amount of the investment, the type of securities being purchased, and any rights or restrictions associated with those securities.

What Is Being Represented?

In the subscription agreement, the investor makes several representations, including that they have reviewed and understood the PPM and that they meet the qualifications required to invest in the offering. These representations protect the company by ensuring that investors acknowledge the risks and terms of the investment.

Signature(s)

The subscription agreement requires the signature of the investor affirming their commitment to the investment. Once signed, the agreement becomes legally binding, and the investor is obligated to provide the funds specified in the agreement.

Issuer Acceptance of the Subscription

After the investor has signed the subscription agreement, the issuer must formally accept the subscription. This acceptance signifies that the issuer has reviewed the investor's suitability and has agreed to issue the securities under the terms outlined in the agreement. Only after the issuer has accepted the subscription does the investment become final.

Next Steps

Once the subscription is accepted, the next steps include finalizing the transfer of funds; issuing the securities to the investor; and providing any necessary post-closing documentation, such as stock certificates or investor account statements. In addition, a warm and gracious "welcome aboard" letter, thanking the investor for their investment, is always a good idea. Maintaining clear communication with the investor throughout this process is essential to ensuring a smooth, professional closing experience.

*   *   *   *   *

The process of onboarding investors through subscription documents and related agreements is critical to ensuring a smooth, compliant capital raise. Each document from the suitability questionnaire to the subscription agreement plays a vital role in protecting both the company and its investors. By carefully following the outlined steps, you can streamline the subscription process while ensuring that your investors meet eligibility requirements. However, given the legal complexities involved, it's essential to consult with your securities attorney throughout this process. Their expertise will help you navigate potential legal pitfalls and ensure that all documents comply with securities regulations, allowing you to focus on growing your business and raise capital with confidence.

CHAPTER **8**

Marketing Strategies for Raising Capital

Raising capital is not only about finding the right investors but also about effectively marketing your business and its investment opportunity. In this chapter, we'll explore marketing strategies that entrepreneurs can use to attract and engage investors from crafting compelling investment narratives to leveraging digital marketing channels. We'll also look at how to remain compliant with securities laws while promoting your offering.

Understanding the Capital Raising Landscape

Overview of Different Types of Capital Raising Methods (e.g., Equity Financing, Debt Financing, Crowdfunding)

When planning your capital raise, it's essential to first understand the various methods available. Equity financing involves selling ownership in your company, whereas debt financing raises capital by borrowing money that will be repaid with interest. Crowdfunding allows businesses to raise smaller amounts of capital from a large group of people in exchange for equity or as donations in reward-based or preorder campaigns. Each method has its own advantages and trade-offs, depending on your company's needs and the type of investors you're targeting.

Key Considerations When Choosing the Right Approach for Your Business

The right approach to raising capital will depend on factors like your business's stage of growth, the amount of funding you need, and your long-term goals. For example, early-stage start-ups might benefit from crowdfunding or angel investors, whereas later-stage companies might turn to VC or private equity. It's important to assess the pros and cons of each method and choose one that aligns with your business's financial and operational goals.

Identifying Your Target Investors

Defining Your Ideal Investor Profile

A critical first step in any capital-raising marketing strategy is identifying your target investors. What type of investor is the best fit for your business? This could range from individual angel investors and VC firms to institutional investors like pension funds or family offices. Your ideal investor will depend on factors like your industry, the amount of capital you're seeking, and the stage of your business. Defining your ideal investor profile allows you to tailor your messaging and outreach efforts accordingly.

Segmenting and Targeting Potential Investors Based on Their Interests and Investment Preferences

Once you have a clear idea of who your ideal investors are, you can begin segmenting and targeting them based on their interests, investment size, and risk tolerance. Investors often have specific preferences such as a focus on early-stage technology companies or an interest in socially responsible investing. By understanding these preferences, you can create targeted marketing campaigns that resonate with different investor segments, increasing your chances of securing capital.

Building Your Investor Network

Strategies for Expanding Your Network of Potential Investors

Building a strong network of potential investors takes time and effort. You can expand your network by attending industry events, joining investor-focused platforms, and leveraging your existing contacts to get warm introductions to investors. Participating in pitch competitions or start-up accelerators can also help you meet investors who are actively seeking new opportunities.

Leveraging Industry Events, Networking Platforms, and Investor Databases

Industry events and conferences are excellent opportunities to meet potential investors face-to-face and build relationships. Online platforms like AngelList, LinkedIn, and Gust provide valuable tools for connecting with investors and presenting your business. Additionally, investor databases and services offered by investor relations firms can help you identify and reach out to the right people. It's essential to approach networking with the mindset of building long-term relationships rather than seeking immediate funding.

Crafting a Compelling Investment Story

Creating a Clear, Persuasive Narrative About Your Business and Investment Opportunity

Investors are drawn to stories, and your investment story needs to be clear and compelling. This narrative should communicate not only what your business does but also why it matters and how it is positioned to grow. Focus on your company's mission, the problem you are solving, and why your solution is unique. A strong narrative creates an emotional connection, making investors more likely to believe in your vision.

Highlighting Key Value Propositions and Growth Potential

A key part of your investment story is highlighting your company's value proposition. What makes your product or service unique? How does it stand out from competitors? It's also crucial to showcase your growth potential by providing data on market size, projected revenue growth, and future expansion plans. Investors want to see a clear path to scale and profitability, so providing them with solid numbers and realistic projections is essential.

Using Digital Marketing Channels

Leveraging Social Media, Email Marketing, and Content Marketing to Reach Investors

Digital marketing channels offer powerful tools for reaching a wide audience of potential investors. Social media platforms like LinkedIn and Twitter allow you to share updates about your business, engage with industry leaders, and build an online presence. Email marketing can help you nurture relationships with interested investors by providing regular updates, financial reports, and key milestones. Content marketing such as blog posts, white papers, and webinars can establish your expertise and keep investors engaged with your company's progress.

Best Practices for Creating Engaging and Compliant Marketing Materials

When marketing your investment opportunity, it's essential to strike a balance between engaging content and legal compliance. Marketing materials should be clear, informative, and compelling, and they must comply with securities regulations. Avoid making exaggerated claims or promises about future returns, and ensure that all disclosures are accurate and transparent. Including disclaimers that remind investors of the risks involved in the offering is a crucial part of staying compliant.

Investor Relations and Engagement

Nurturing Relationships with Existing and Potential Investors

Building strong relationships with your investors is key to long-term success. Investor relations should be viewed as an ongoing process, not just something that happens during the fundraising phase. Keep investors informed about your company's progress, and regularly communicate important milestones, financial updates, and strategic decisions. Providing transparency and fostering trust will help maintain investor confidence, making it easier to raise future capital.

Providing Timely Updates and Communication to Maintain Investor Confidence

Timely communication is critical for maintaining investor confidence. Keep your investors updated on both successes and challenges. Regular reports such as quarterly financial updates and progress reports help reassure investors that their capital is being managed responsibly. It's also important to respond promptly to investor inquiries and feedback demonstrating that you value their involvement in your company's growth.

Compliance and Regulatory Considerations

Ensuring Marketing Efforts Comply with Securities Laws and Regulations

Marketing securities offerings comes with a host of regulatory requirements. Private placements, for example, are subject to strict rules about who can be solicited and how offers can be made. Regulation D, particularly Rules 506(b) and 506(c), has specific guidelines on investor solicitation and accredited investor verification. Ensure that all your marketing efforts comply with these regulations to avoid penalties or jeopardizing the legality of your capital raise.

Reviewing Advertising Restrictions and Disclaimers

When marketing your investment opportunity, be sure to include the appropriate disclaimers. These disclaimers inform potential investors that the securities being offered are subject to legal restrictions and are not registered with the SEC. For example, advertisements for Regulation D Rule 506(c) offerings must include disclaimers stating that the securities are offered only to accredited investors. Also, Reg CF advertisements are limited to "tombstone" ads, which much direct the investor to the issuer's crowdfunding portal for additional information.

Above all, avoid making misleading or overly optimistic statements about potential returns.

Measuring and Evaluating Marketing Effectiveness

Metrics for Assessing the Success of Marketing Campaigns

As with any marketing campaign, it's important to track metrics that indicate the success of your investor outreach efforts. Metrics might include the number of investor inquiries received, the conversion rate of inquiries to actual investments, and the level of engagement on social media or email campaigns. Measuring these key performance indicators (KPIs) allows you to assess what's working and where improvements are needed.

Making Data-Driven Decisions to Optimize Future Efforts

Once you have data from responses to your initial marketing campaigns, you can make adjustments to improve future efforts. If certain marketing channels, such as email or social media, are driving more investor interest than others, allocate more resources to those areas. By making data-driven decisions, you can refine your marketing strategies and increase the likelihood of securing the capital your business needs.

* * * * *

Effective marketing strategies are essential to raising capital and building lasting relationships with potential investors. By using digital marketing channels, creating compelling investment narratives, and maintaining transparency in all communications, you can attract the right investors to your offering. However, marketing efforts in the capital-raising process must be carefully aligned with securities laws and regulatory requirements. As you develop your marketing strategy, you must work closely with your securities attorney to ensure that your materials are compliant and legally sound. Their guidance will help protect your business while allowing you to reach your fundraising goals with confidence.

CHAPTER 9

Brokers, Finders, and Other Money Raisers

Entrepreneurs raising capital have several options when it comes to working with professionals who can help connect them with investors. From broker–dealers and placement agents to finders and other inter-mediaries, each option comes with its own set of benefits, risks, and legal considerations. This chapter will provide an in-depth look at the various money raisers entrepreneurs can leverage along with the com-pliance issues and costs associated with each.

Using Broker–Dealers to Raise Capital

Defining the Role of Broker–Dealers in Raising Capital

"Broker–dealers" are registered entities that facilitate the buying and selling of securities on behalf of clients. In the context of raising capi-tal, broker–dealers can act as intermediaries connecting businesses with potential investors. Their role may include marketing securities, negotiating terms, and closing deals. Broker–dealers are regulated by FINRA and the SEC to ensure that they operate within the framework of securities laws.

Understanding the Regulatory Landscape for Broker–Dealers

Broker–dealers are subject to strict regulations that govern their activities. They must be licensed and registered with both FINRA and the SEC, and they must comply with rules designed to protect investors and maintain market integrity. These regulations include requirements around disclosures, conflict-of-interest management, and maintaining accurate records. Entrepreneurs working with broker–dealers should ensure that the broker–dealer is fully compliant and in good standing with regulatory authorities.

Pros and Cons of Engaging Broker–Dealers in the Fundraising Process

The primary advantage of working with a broker–dealer is their access to a wide network of investors. Broker–dealers often have established relationships with institutional investors, family offices, and high-net-worth individuals. Additionally, their experience in negotiating and structuring deals can provide value to entrepreneurs who may be unfamiliar with the complexities of capital raising. However, broker–dealers typically charge significant fees that can range from 5% to 10% of the capital raised. These fees can be a substantial cost for start-ups or smaller businesses, making it important to weigh the potential benefits against the financial burden.

Understanding Placement Agents

Defining the Role of Placement Agents in Capital Raising

Placement agents are professionals who specialize in raising capital for private investment funds such as private equity or VC funds. They act as intermediaries between the fund and potential investors helping to secure commitments from institutions or high-net-worth individuals. Placement agents typically work on a commission basis receiving a percentage of the total funds raised.

Differentiating Placement Agents from Brokers and Finders

While placement agents and broker–dealers have similarities, placement agents tend to focus on private placements rather than public offerings. Unlike broker–dealers, placement agents are not usually involved in the broader buying and selling of securities. Additionally, placement agents are more likely to work exclusively with institutional investors, whereas broker–dealers may engage with a broader range of investors, including retail clients. Finders, meanwhile, are individuals or firms that introduce potential investors to issuers but do not negotiate or close deals.

Compliance Considerations When Working with Placement Agents

Working with placement agents requires strict adherence to securities laws because placement agents must be registered with FINRA or exempt from registration in specific situations. Placement agents also need to comply with regulations around disclosures, marketing materials, and investor communications. It's essential for entrepreneurs to conduct due diligence on placement agents to ensure they are reputable and compliant with all legal requirements.

Leveraging Finders and Intermediaries

Differentiating Finders from Broker–Dealers, Placement Agents, and Other Intermediaries

Finders play a more limited role in capital raising compared to broker–dealers and placement agents. A finder's job is typically to make introductions between investors and companies seeking capital. They do not negotiate deals, close transactions, or participate in ongoing communications with investors. The use of finders is common in early-stage fundraising, particularly among start-ups and small businesses that may not yet have access to large networks of institutional investors.

Identifying the Benefits and Risks of Using Finders in Capital Raising

One of the main benefits of using finders is their ability to introduce companies to potential investors at a lower cost than broker–dealers or placement agents. Finders often charge a flat fee or a small percentage of the funds raised, making them a cost-effective option for start-ups. However, because finders are not typically registered with regulatory bodies like FINRA, they may operate in a legally gray area. This can pose risks for both the company and the investors if the finder's activities are later deemed to violate securities laws.

> *One of the main benefits of using finders is their ability to introduce companies to potential investors at a lower cost than broker–dealers or placement agents ... However, because finders are not typically registered with regulatory bodies like FINRA, they may operate in a legally gray area.*

Complying with Applicable Laws and Regulations When Working with Finders

Regulatory authorities like the SEC have strict rules around who can receive compensation for raising capital. While finders are often exempt from registration as broker–dealers, their activities must still comply with securities laws. Entrepreneurs should ensure that the finder's role is limited to making introductions and that they are not engaging in activities that would require them to be registered as a broker–dealer. It's important to consult legal counsel before engaging finders to ensure full compliance.

Considering Other Money Raisers

Exploring Alternative Methods of Raising Capital

In addition to broker–dealers, placement agents, and finders, there are other methods of raising capital that entrepreneurs can explore. These include online platforms, crowdfunding, and direct-to-investor strategies. Each method has its own set of advantages, depending on the stage of the company and the type of investors being targeted. For example, crowdfunding platforms allow businesses to raise smaller amounts of capital from a large number of investors, whereas direct-to-investor strategies involve reaching out to investors individually.

Crowdfunding Platforms and Their Role in Capital Raising

Crowdfunding platforms like Kickstarter, Republic, and SeedInvest provide an alternative to traditional fundraising methods. These platforms enable companies to raise capital from a large pool of investors, including both accredited and non-accredited investors depending on the platform and offering type. Reg CF allows companies to raise up to $5 million from the public in a 12-month period, but this method requires strict adherence to SEC regulations regarding disclosures and investor protections.

Evaluating the Effectiveness of Different Money Raisers

The effectiveness of different capital-raising methods depends on the company's goals, target investor base, and the amount of capital needed. Broker–dealers and placement agents are often best for companies seeking to raise large amounts of capital from institutional investors, whereas crowdfunding can be effective for smaller raises or for companies looking to engage a broader audience of retail investors. Entrepreneurs should evaluate each option carefully to determine which is the best fit for their needs.

Legal and Regulatory Compliance

Understanding Securities Laws and Regulations Related to Capital Raising

Whether working with broker–dealers, placement agents, or finders, entrepreneurs must ensure that their capital-raising efforts comply with federal and state securities laws. The SEC's Regulation D, which governs private placements, is a key regulation to understand. It includes provisions on accredited investor verification, advertising restrictions, and exemptions from registration. Companies must also be aware of blue sky laws, which are state-specific securities regulations.

Compliance Requirements for Broker–Dealers, Placement Agents, Finders, and Other Intermediaries

Each type of intermediary in the capital-raising process has its own set of compliance requirements. Broker–dealers must be registered with FINRA and comply with federal securities laws, and placement agents may also need to be registered depending on their activities. Finders may not need to be registered, but they still must operate within the boundaries of securities regulations. Entrepreneurs should work closely with legal counsel to ensure that all intermediaries involved in their capital raise are compliant with applicable laws.

Best Practices for Ensuring Compliance Throughout the Fundraising Process

To ensure compliance, entrepreneurs should establish clear processes for vetting and working with intermediaries. This includes conducting due diligence on broker–dealers, placement agents, and finders as well as consulting legal professionals to review all contracts and agreements. It's also important to maintain accurate records of all communications with investors and intermediaries because these records may be required in the event of a regulatory inquiry.

Evaluating the Costs and Benefits

Analyzing the Financial Implications of Engaging Brokers, Placement Agents, Finders, and Other Money Raisers

The costs of engaging intermediaries in the capital-raising process can vary widely. Broker–dealers and placement agents typically charge a percentage of the total capital raised, often between 5% and 10%. Finders usually charge lower fees, but their involvement is more limited. Crowdfunding platforms often charge fees based on the total amount raised plus additional costs for marketing and compliance services. Entrepreneurs must carefully evaluate the financial implications of these fees and weigh them against the potential benefits of working with intermediaries.

Assessing the Value They Bring to the Fundraising Effort

While intermediaries can provide access to investor networks and help manage the complexities of the fundraising process, not all intermediaries add the same level of value. Broker–dealers, for example, can offer strategic advice, deal structuring expertise, and regulatory guidance, whereas finders may only make introductions. Entrepreneurs should assess whether the value provided by the intermediary justifies the cost and whether the intermediary's expertise aligns with the company's fundraising goals.

* * * * *

As discussed, engaging brokers, finders, and other intermediaries can be a powerful way to enhance your capital-raising efforts. However, navigating the legal requirements and understanding the differences between these roles is essential to avoid potential pitfalls. Each intermediary brings different value and risks to the process, and their involvement must comply with applicable securities regulations. As you explore these relationships, it's crucial to involve your securities attorney early on to ensure all agreements and interactions are legally compliant and strategically sound. With the right legal counsel by your side, you can make informed decisions and structure your capital-raising process effectively.

CHAPTER **10**

Raising Capital Legally Via Social Media

With the rise of digital platforms, social media has become an increasingly powerful tool for raising capital. Entrepreneurs can now reach a global audience of potential investors, fostering relationships, and driving interest in their business. However, using social media for capital raising comes with legal considerations, particularly in the context of securities laws and general solicitation rules. In this chapter, we will explore how to navigate these challenges and effectively raise capital through social media while bearing in mind that only a limited number of exemptions (i.e., Rule 506(c) of Regulation D and Reg CF) outside of registration with the SEC permit such strategies.

Understanding Social Media as a Capital-Raising Tool

Overview of Popular Social Media Platforms for Engaging Potential Investors

Social media platforms such as LinkedIn, Twitter, Facebook, and

Instagram provide unparalleled opportunities for reaching investors. Each platform offers unique features and audiences, making it essential to choose the right one for your capital-raising strategy. LinkedIn, for example, is ideal for reaching professional investors, VCs, and angel investors because of its business-oriented network. Twitter can be used to engage in industry conversations, whereas Instagram and Facebook are useful for building brand awareness and engaging a broader audience through visual storytelling.

Exploring the Benefits and Challenges of Using Social Media for Capital Raising

The primary benefit of using social media to raise capital is the ability to quickly and cost-effectively reach a vast, diverse audience. Social media allows businesses to engage with potential investors directly, build relationships, and increase visibility for their fundraising efforts. However, there are challenges as well, including the risk of violating securities regulations, managing public perception, and ensuring that messaging remains compliant with the law. Entrepreneurs must strike a balance between promoting their business and adhering to legal constraints.

Legal Considerations and Compliance

Reviewing Securities Laws and Regulations Related to Soliciting Investors on Social Media

When using social media to raise capital, it's important to understand the legal restrictions around general solicitation and advertising of securities. In the US, securities offerings are subject to regulations such as the Securities Act of 1933, which imposes restrictions on how and to whom securities can be offered. For example, Regulation D Rule 506(b) prohibits general solicitation meaning that companies cannot publicly advertise their offering to non-accredited investors. However, Rule 506(c) allows general solicitation but limits participation to verified accredited investors. Entrepreneurs must be aware of these rules to avoid legal penalties.

Understanding the JOBS Act and Its Impact on Crowdfunding and General Solicitation

The Jumpstart Our Business Startups (JOBS) Act, passed in 2012, revolutionized how businesses can raise capital through social media and crowdfunding. Title II of the JOBS Act allows companies to use general solicitation to reach accredited investors under Rule 506(c). Title III, known as Reg CF, permits companies to raise capital from both accredited and non-accredited investors, provided the offering is conducted through a registered crowdfunding portal. These changes have made it easier for entrepreneurs to promote their offerings on social media while remaining compliant with securities laws.

Compliance Best Practices to Avoid Legal Pitfalls and Consequences

To avoid legal risks, companies should implement best practices for social media compliance. This includes using clear disclaimers that inform potential investors of the risks associated with the investment, ensuring that communications do not include misleading or exaggerated claims, and verifying the accreditation of investors before accepting funds. Companies should also avoid making public statements about specific investment terms on platforms where they might be seen by non-accredited investors unless operating under Reg CF or Rule 506(c).

Identifying and Targeting Potential Investors

Defining Your Target Audience and Investor Personas

Successful capital raising through social media begins with identifying your target audience. This includes defining investor personas based on factors such as investment size, risk tolerance, industry focus, and geographic location. For example, angel investors may be interested in early-stage start-ups with high growth potential, whereas institutional investors may focus on later-stage companies. Tailoring your social media strategy to the specific needs and preferences of these investor groups is crucial for maximizing engagement.

Segmenting and Tailoring Messages for Different Social Media Platforms

Each social media platform attracts a different audience, so your messaging must be tailored accordingly. On LinkedIn, you might focus on sharing detailed business updates, industry insights, and professional achievements to engage with investors. On Instagram or Facebook, storytelling through visuals and videos might be more effective in showcasing the human side of your business and its growth potential. Segmenting your messages allows you to speak directly to the unique interests of each platform's users.

Crafting Engaging and Compliant Content

Creating Compelling Content That Adheres to Securities Regulations

Creating engaging content that captures investor interest is key to social media success, but this content must also be compliant with securities laws. Avoid making specific promises about returns or issuing misleading statements about the investment opportunity. Instead, focus on providing informative content that educates potential investors about your business, its mission, and its market opportunity. Be transparent about risks and ensure that all communications are accurate and balanced.

Balancing Promotional Messaging with Informative and Educational Content

When raising capital on social media, it's important to strike a balance between promotional and educational content. Overly promotional messaging can appear untrustworthy, whereas informative content helps build credibility and trust. Share insights into your industry, explain your business model, and provide thought leadership to position your company as a knowledgeable and credible investment opportunity. Providing educational content also helps you comply with regulations that prohibit misleading or exaggerated claims.

> *When raising capital on social media, it's important to strike a balance between promotional and educational content. Overly promotional messaging can appear untrustworthy, whereas informative content helps build credibility and trust.*

Using Visuals, Videos, and Storytelling to Capture Investor Interest

Visual content is a powerful tool for engaging potential investors on social media. Use visuals to showcase your products, services, team, or progress. Videos can be particularly effective, allowing you to tell your company's story in a dynamic and engaging way. Whether it's a behind-the-scenes look at your operations or a testimonial from an existing investor, visual content can help bring your investment opportunity to life and create a deeper connection with potential investors.

Building an Online Presence and Credibility

Establishing a Credible Brand Presence on Social Media

Building a strong, credible online presence is essential for attracting investors. This includes maintaining consistent branding across all social media platforms, posting regularly, and engaging with your audience in a professional and thoughtful manner. Showcasing your expertise and demonstrating your knowledge of the industry will help establish your credibility, making investors more likely to trust your business and consider investing.

Showcasing Past Successes, Testimonials, and Positive Investor Experiences

One of the most effective ways to build credibility with potential investors is to showcase past successes. Share testimonials from current investors, highlight major milestones or achievements, and provide case studies that demonstrate your company's growth and potential. Positive investor experiences can go a long way in reassuring potential investors that your business is a sound investment.

Engaging with Your Audience and Responding to Inquiries Professionally

Social media is a two-way communication channel, so it's important to engage with your audience and respond to inquiries promptly and professionally. Whether it's answering questions, responding to comments, or addressing concerns, engaging with potential investors shows that you value their interest and are committed to transparency. Handling communication effectively helps build trust and can lead to stronger relationships with investors.

Measuring and Analyzing Social Media Impact

Identifying Key Performance Indicators for Social Media Campaigns

To evaluate the success of your social media efforts, you need to establish KPIs that measure engagement and impact. These might include metrics such as the number of investor inquiries generated, the level of engagement (e.g., likes, comments, shares), and the conversion rate of social media leads into actual investments. Tracking these KPIs allows you to measure the effectiveness of your campaigns and make informed decisions about future strategies.

Using Analytics Tools to Track Engagement, Leads, and Conversions

Platforms such as LinkedIn, Facebook, and Twitter offer analytics tools that provide valuable insights into how your content is performing. Use these tools to track the number of views, clicks, and interactions your posts receive and monitor how many leads are generated through social media. Analyzing these data helps you understand what types of content resonate most with investors and where you may need to adjust your strategy.

Making Data-Driven Decisions to Optimize Social Media Efforts

By analyzing the data from your social media campaigns, you can make informed decisions about how to optimize your efforts. If certain types of content or platforms are driving more engagement and leads, consider focusing more of your resources on those areas. Regularly reviewing and adjusting your social media strategy based on data-driven insights can help improve the effectiveness of your capital-raising efforts.

Leveraging Crowdfunding and Social Media Synergy

Exploring the Connection Between Crowdfunding Campaigns and Social Media Marketing

Social media and crowdfunding go hand-in-hand when it comes to raising capital. Many successful crowdfunding campaigns owe much of their success to effective social media marketing. By promoting your crowdfunding campaign on social media, you can increase visibility, attract more investors, and create a sense of community around your project. Social media platforms allow you to share campaign updates, engage with backers, and build momentum throughout the fundraising process.

Crowdfunding Projects That Used Social Media Effectively

There are many examples of companies using social media to successfully raise capital through crowdfunding. From product launches on Kickstarter to equity crowdfunding on platforms like SeedInvest, businesses have used social media to reach a broader audience and drive interest in their campaigns. These success stories demonstrate the power of combining social media marketing with crowdfunding to achieve fundraising goals.

Mitigating Risks and Addressing Challenges

Handling Negative Feedback or Criticism on Social Media

Negative feedback or criticism on social media is inevitable, so how you handle it can make a big difference. It's important to respond professionally and address any concerns raised by your audience. Avoid getting defensive or confrontational, and instead use negative feedback as an opportunity to show transparency and improve your relationship with potential investors. A thoughtful response can turn criticism into a positive interaction.

Dealing with Potential Privacy and Security Concerns

Raising capital through social media involves sharing information publicly, which can raise privacy and security concerns. Be mindful of the information you share, and ensure that sensitive data such as financial details or investor information are kept secure. Use secure platforms for any investor communications that involve private or confidential information, and ensure that your social media profiles are properly protected against hacking or unauthorized access.

Avoiding Common Mistakes and Risks Associated with Social Media Use

Common mistakes when using social media to raise capital include making exaggerated claims, failing to comply with securities regulations, and neglecting to engage with your audience. Entrepreneurs should take care to avoid these pitfalls by ensuring that all content is compliant, accurate, and well-targeted. Consistent engagement and maintaining a professional presence will also help mitigate risks and improve the effectiveness of your capital-raising efforts.

* * * * *

Leveraging social media as part of your capital-raising strategy offers tremendous potential, but it must be approached with care and compliance. Social media provides a powerful platform to reach a broader audience of potential investors, but it also introduces additional regulatory challenges. Ensuring that your social media communications adhere to securities laws and regulations is critical to avoiding potential legal issues. Working closely with your securities attorney will help you create compliant and effective social media campaigns, allowing you to maximize your outreach while staying within the bounds of the law. With the right approach, social media can be a powerful tool in your fundraising efforts.

CHAPTER **11**

Public Offerings vs. Private Offerings

When raising capital, businesses often must choose between conducting a public or private offering. Both options present unique opportunities, challenges, and regulatory requirements. In this chapter, we'll compare public and private offerings in terms of their characteristics, regulatory landscape, investor profiles, costs, and other critical factors. Understanding these differences will help entrepreneurs determine the best approach for their capital-raising needs.

Public Offerings

Defining Public Offerings and Their Characteristics

A public offering is a process by which a company offers its securities such as stocks or bonds to the public on the open market. The most well-known type of public offering is an IPO, where a private company sells shares to institutional and retail investors for the first time. After the IPO, the company's shares are traded on a stock exchange. Public offerings are subject to strict regulatory oversight with companies required to register their securities with the SEC and provide extensive disclosures to the public.

Exploring Different Types of Public Offerings (e.g., IPOs, Follow-On Offerings, Regulation A)

In addition to IPOs, there are other types of public offerings that companies can pursue. Follow-on offerings, also known as secondary offerings, occur when a public company issues additional shares after its IPO. Another option is Regulation A, which allows smaller companies to raise up to $75 million from the public without going through the full IPO process. Regulation A is particularly useful for companies that want to access public capital markets without the costs and complexities of a traditional IPO.

Highlighting Advantages and Challenges of Going Public

Going public has several advantages, including access to a broader pool of capital, increased liquidity for shareholders, and enhanced visibility and credibility. Public companies can raise large sums of money quickly, and their shares can be used as currency for acquisitions or employee compensation. However, the challenges of going public include extensive regulatory requirements, ongoing disclosure obligations, and significant costs. Public companies are also subject to market volatility, which can impact their stock price and overall valuation.

Private Offerings

Defining Private Offerings and Their Characteristics

A private offering involves the sale of securities to a select group of accredited investors, institutions, or high-net-worth individuals rather than to the general public. Private offerings are not subject to the same regulatory scrutiny as public offerings, and they typically rely on exemptions from SEC registration such as Regulation D. Because private offerings are limited to accredited investors, they offer more flexibility in terms of structuring the deal and negotiating terms with investors.

Examining Common Types of Private Offerings (e.g., Regulation D, Regulation Crowdfunding)

Private offerings can take various forms depending on the type of exemption used. Regulation D, specifically Rules 506(b) and 506(c), is one of the most common exemptions for private placements allowing companies to raise unlimited capital from accredited investors. Rule 506(c) also permits general solicitation, provided that all investors are verified as accredited. Reg CF, meanwhile, allows companies to raise up to $5 million from both accredited and non-accredited investors, making it a popular option for start-ups and small businesses seeking smaller amounts of capital.

Discussing Benefits and Considerations of Private Placements

The benefits of private placements include faster execution, fewer regulatory hurdles, and greater flexibility in negotiating terms with investors. Private companies can maintain control over their business and avoid the public scrutiny that comes with being listed on an exchange. However, private placements typically limit the pool of potential investors to accredited individuals or institutions, which may reduce the amount of capital that can be raised. Additionally, private offerings often come with less liquidity for investors because there is no public market for the securities.

Regulatory Landscape and Compliance

Comparing the Regulatory Requirements for Public and Private Offerings

Public offerings are highly regulated and require companies to register their securities with the SEC, file a prospectus, and adhere to ongoing reporting obligations under the Securities Exchange Act of 1934. Private offerings benefit from various exemptions from SEC registration such as Regulation D or Regulation A. While private offerings are less burdensome from a regulatory perspective, they still require compliance with certain rules, including verifying investor accreditation and providing adequate disclosures to investors.

Addressing the Role of the Securities and Exchange Commission

The SEC plays a critical role in overseeing both public and private offerings. For public offerings, the SEC requires companies to file a registration statement (Form S-1) and provide extensive disclosures about their business, finances, and risk factors. For private offerings, the SEC's role is to ensure that companies comply with the exemptions under Regulation D, Regulation A, or Reg CF. Failure to comply with SEC regulations can result in penalties, fines, or the unwinding of the offering.

Emphasizing the Importance of Adhering to Securities Laws and Regulations

Whether pursuing a public or private offering, adherence to securities laws is paramount. Companies must ensure that all marketing materials, investor communications, and offering documents comply with applicable laws. In private offerings, this includes providing accurate disclosures to investors and verifying accreditation status where required. Noncompliance with securities laws can lead to severe legal consequences, including civil liabilities, SEC enforcement actions, and damage to the company's reputation.

Investor Profiles and Reach

Analyzing the Difference in Investor Profiles Between Public and Private Offerings

Public offerings provide greater accessibility to the average investor because shares are traded on public exchanges, and anyone can purchase them.

Private offerings ... often offer more flexibility in deal structuring and investor terms, allowing companies to negotiate directly with investors.

Public offerings typically attract a broad range of investors, from institutional investors like pension funds and mutual funds to retail investors. This diversity allows companies to access a larger pool of capital and build a diverse shareholder base. Private offerings, by contrast, are limited to accredited investors or qualified institutions. These investors tend to have higher risk tolerance and are more familiar with the complexities of private equity investing. However, the limited pool of investors can make it more challenging for private companies to raise large sums of capital.

Exploring the Accessibility of Investors in Public vs. Private Offerings

Public offerings provide greater accessibility to the average investor because shares are traded on public exchanges, and anyone can purchase them. Private offerings are generally restricted to a select group of investors, limiting access to only those who meet specific financial criteria. While private offerings may be more exclusive, they often offer more flexibility in deal structuring and investor terms, allowing companies to negotiate directly with investors.

Evaluating the Impact of Offering Size on Investor Participation

The size of the offering can also impact investor participation. Public offerings are typically used to raise large sums of capital, often in the hundreds of millions or billions of dollars. Private offerings, while more flexible, are generally used to raise smaller amounts of capital though some private placements can still raise significant sums, especially in later-stage venture rounds or private equity deals. The size of the offering influences the types of investors involved, with institutional investors often participating in larger offerings, whereas smaller offerings may attract individual accredited investors.

Disclosure and Transparency

Discussing the Level of Disclosure Required in Public Offerings

Public offerings require extensive disclosures to ensure that investors have all the information they need to make informed decisions. Companies must file a prospectus with the SEC outlining details about their financials, business operations, risks, and future growth strategies. These disclosures are subject to review by the SEC, and any material omissions or misstatements can result in penalties or litigation.

Comparing Disclosure Requirements in Private Offerings

Private offerings have more relaxed disclosure requirements than do public offerings, but companies are still required to provide material information to investors. This typically includes financial statements, a description of the business, and any significant risks associated with the investment. Private companies often use PPMs to disclose this information to potential investors. While the disclosures may be less extensive than in public offerings, they must still be accurate and comply with securities laws.

Exploring How Transparency Affects Investor Confidence

Transparency is a key factor in building investor confidence whether in a public or private offering. Investors are more likely to invest in a company that provides clear, honest, and comprehensive information about its operations, financials, and risks. In public offerings, transparency is enforced through mandatory disclosures and ongoing reporting requirements. In private offerings, companies must still be transparent, particularly when it comes to risk factors and financial health, to avoid legal liabilities and foster investor trust.

Timeline and Costs

Highlighting the Timeline of IPOs, Including the Registration Process

The timeline for a public offering or IPO is long, often taking several months to a year from the initial decision to go public to the actual sale of shares. The registration process with the SEC is rigorous, requiring companies to prepare and file detailed documents, undergo audits, and respond to SEC comments. Additionally, companies must conduct roadshows to market the offering to potential investors. This extended timeline can delay access to capital, making public offerings less appealing for companies that need funding quickly.

Examining the Speed of Execution in Private Offerings

Private offerings are typically faster to execute than public offerings because they are not subject to the same level of regulatory scrutiny.

Companies can often raise capital within weeks or a few months, depending on the complexity of the deal and the number of investors involved. The streamlined process of private placements makes them an attractive option for companies seeking quick access to capital without the lengthy registration process required in public markets.

Analyzing the Costs Associated with Both Types of Offerings

Public offerings are significantly more expensive than private offerings due to the costs of SEC registration, legal fees, underwriting fees, and ongoing compliance costs. In contrast, private offerings have lower up-front costs because they are exempt from many of the regulatory requirements that apply to public offerings. However, private placements still involve legal and accounting fees as well as costs related to marketing the offering to potential investors.

Liquidity and Exit Strategies

Addressing the Liquidity Options Available to Investors in Public Offerings

One of the main advantages of public offerings is the liquidity they provide to investors. Once a company's shares are listed on a stock exchange, investors can buy and sell shares, freely giving them the flexibility to exit their investment at any time. This liquidity is particularly appealing to institutional investors and retail investors who want the option to trade their shares on the open market.

Discussing Exit Strategies for Private Offering Investors

Private offering investors have more limited liquidity options. Because there is no public market for private securities, investors may need to wait for a liquidity event such as an acquisition, merger, or IPO to exit their investment. In some cases, private companies may offer secondary sales of shares, allowing investors to sell their stakes to other private investors. However, these transactions are often subject to restrictions and may require approval from the company's management.

Understanding the Implications of Liquidity on Investor Decisions

The liquidity (or lack thereof) associated with an offering can have a significant impact on investor decisions. Public offerings provide immediate liquidity, making them attractive to investors who prefer flexibility. Private offerings, while potentially offering higher returns, come with the risk of illiquidity because investors may be locked into their investment for several years. Understanding these implications is crucial for both entrepreneurs and investors when structuring deals and making investment decisions.

* * * * *

Successfully navigating the decision between public and private offerings requires a deep understanding of your business's goals and growth trajectory as well as the regulatory landscape. Public offerings provide greater access to capital and liquidity but come with increased regulatory burdens and disclosure requirements. In contrast, private offerings offer flexibility and reduced oversight but limit the pool of investors and liquidity options. Careful consideration of the type of investors you wish to attract, the level of transparency you are willing to provide, and the costs associated with each path is essential. Engaging with experienced securities counsel will help you make the best choice for your company and ensure compliance with the complex legal frameworks governing both types of offerings. With the right approach, you can raise the necessary capital while positioning your business for long-term success.

CHAPTER **12**

Succeeding with Federal and State Securities Regulators

Raising capital requires compliance with a complex web of federal and state securities laws designed to protect investors and maintain market integrity. Entrepreneurs must navigate interactions with securities regulators such as the SEC and state regulators enforcing blue sky laws. This chapter will explore how to effectively manage regulatory compliance, communication, and enforcement risks to ensure a smooth capital-raising process.

The Role of Securities Regulators

Defining the Responsibilities of Federal (SEC) and State Securities Regulators (Blue Sky Laws)

Federal and state securities regulators play a crucial role in overseeing securities offerings and ensuring that companies comply with laws designed to protect investors. The SEC is the primary federal agency responsible for regulating the securities industry, including public offerings and private placements. The SEC enforces rules established by the

Securities Act of 1933, the Securities Exchange Act of 1934, and other laws. At the state level, securities regulators enforce blue sky laws, which vary from state to state but generally aim to protect investors from fraud and ensure full disclosure.

Exploring Their Roles in Ensuring Investor Protection and Market Integrity

Both federal and state regulators are tasked with ensuring that companies raising capital do so in a way that is transparent, fair, and compliant with securities laws. These regulators monitor for fraudulent activity; ensure that investors have access to material information; and protect the integrity of the market by enforcing strict rules regarding disclosures, registration, and reporting. Their role is to prevent abuses that could harm investors and damage confidence in the financial markets.

Federal Securities Regulations

Overview of the Securities Act of 1933 and Its Key Provisions

The Securities Act of 1933 was enacted to regulate the offer and sale of securities in the United States. The law requires that companies offering securities to the public register their offerings with the SEC unless they qualify for an exemption. The key provisions of the act focus on ensuring that investors receive complete and accurate information about the securities being offered primarily through the filing of a registration statement and prospectus. The act also establishes penalties for fraud and misrepresentation in the sale of securities.

Understanding the Registration Process for Public Offerings

For companies pursuing a public offering, the registration process can be lengthy, complex, and expensive. For example, Regulation A allows companies to raise up to $75 million through a purportedly streamlined SEC registration process, making it an option for smaller businesses who want to access public capital markets without the cost of a traditional IPO. However, companies should plan to spend at least $100,000 in legal and accounting fees to get through the registration process, not including marketing allowances. Companies must file a registration statement (a Form 1-A under Regulation A or a Form S-1 otherwise) with the SEC, which includes detailed information about their business, financial condition, management, and risk factors. The SEC reviews this document to ensure it complies with disclosure requirements and may provide comments or request additional information. Only after the SEC declares the registration effective can the company proceed with the public sale of securities. This process can take several months and requires careful attention to detail.

> *Regulation A allows companies to raise up to $75 million through a purportedly streamlined SEC registration process, making it an option for smaller businesses who want to access public capital markets without the cost of a traditional IPO.*

Exemptions from Registration

While public offerings require registration with the SEC, many companies choose to raise capital through private placements, which can qualify for exemptions from registration under Regulation D or Reg CF. Regulation D, particularly Rule 506(b) and Rule 506(c), allows companies to raise unlimited capital from accredited investors without the need for full SEC registration, provided full disclosure is given via a PPM and the applicable rules are strictly adhered to. Reg CF allows companies to raise up to $5 million from the public in a 12-month period, but this method requires strict adherence to SEC regulations regarding disclosures and investor protections.

State Securities Regulations (Blue Sky Laws)

Exploring the Concept of Blue Sky Laws and Their Purpose

Blue sky laws are state-level securities regulations designed to protect investors from fraudulent or overly speculative investments. Each state has its own set of blue sky laws that can vary in their requirements for registration, exemptions, and disclosures. These laws typically require companies to register their securities offerings with the state before they can be sold to investors within that state. Blue sky laws ensure that investors have access to material information about the investment and prevent the sale of unregulated or misleading securities.

Discussing State-Level Registration and Exemption Requirements

To comply with blue sky laws, companies raising capital through private placements must either register their offering with each state or qualify for an exemption. Some states automatically recognize federal exemptions like Regulation D, whereas others have additional requirements. Entrepreneurs should work closely with legal counsel to determine which states require additional filings, fees, or disclosures. Failure to comply with state regulations can result in penalties or the inability to sell securities in that state.

Challenges and Considerations When Dealing with Multiple State Regulators

Navigating multiple state regulations can be challenging, particularly for companies conducting private offerings across several states. Each state may have its own registration requirements, filing fees, and disclosure obligations. Coordinating compliance with multiple regulators requires careful planning and documentation. Entrepreneurs should be aware of the potential delays and costs associated with state-level compliance and may benefit from working with a specialized securities attorney or compliance firm to streamline the process.

Compliance and Disclosure Obligations

Analyzing the Disclosure Requirements for Securities Offerings

Disclosure is a cornerstone of securities regulation. Both public and private offerings require companies to provide potential investors with all material information about the business including financial statements, risk factors, and the terms of the offering. Public companies must comply with ongoing disclosure obligations, including filing quarterly and annual reports with the SEC. In private offerings, companies often use PPMs to disclose material information to investors, ensuring that they understand the risks and rewards associated with the investment.

Ongoing Reporting Obligations for Public Companies

For companies that go public, the regulatory burden doesn't end after the IPO. Public companies must comply with ongoing reporting obligations under the Securities Exchange Act of 1934. This includes filing annual reports (Form 10-K), quarterly reports (Form 10-Q), and current reports (Form 8-K) for significant events. These reports provide investors with up-to-date information about the company's financial health, operations, and management. Failure to meet these reporting requirements can result in penalties, fines, or even the delisting of the company's shares from a public exchange.

Tips for Crafting Accurate, Comprehensive Disclosure Documents

When preparing disclosure documents, accuracy and completeness are critical. Companies must ensure that all material information is disclosed and that the language used is clear and understandable. Disclosures should provide a balanced view of the company's business highlighting both opportunities and risks. It's important to avoid overly optimistic projections or making claims that cannot be substantiated. Working with experienced legal counsel is essential to ensure that disclosures meet regulatory standards and protect the company from potential legal liabilities.

Interaction with Regulators

Navigating Communications with the SEC and State Regulators

Interacting with securities regulators requires professionalism, transparency, and responsiveness. Whether dealing with the SEC or state regulators, it's important to provide accurate information and respond to inquiries in a timely manner. Regulators may request additional documentation, ask for clarifications, or initiate an investigation if they suspect noncompliance. Maintaining open and cooperative communication with regulators can help resolve issues more efficiently and reduce the likelihood of enforcement actions.

Addressing Inquiries, Requests for Information, and Enforcement Actions

If a company receives an inquiry or request for information from the SEC or state regulators, it's essential to take the matter seriously. These requests often indicate that the regulator has concerns about the company's compliance with securities laws. Companies should respond promptly and thoroughly providing all requested information and cooperating fully with the investigation. In cases where the company is subject to an enforcement action such as a cease-and-desist order or civil penalty, it's critical to work with legal counsel to address the issue and mitigate potential consequences.

Best Practices for Maintaining Positive Relationships with Regulators

Building and maintaining positive relationships with regulators can make the compliance process smooth and reduce the risk of enforcement actions. Companies should prioritize transparency and proactive communication with regulators to keep them informed of significant developments and ensure that all filings are accurate and timely. Regularly reviewing compliance procedures and staying up-to-date with regulatory changes can also help maintain a positive relationship with regulators.

Legal and Regulatory Updates

Staying Informed About Changes in Securities Laws and Regulations

Securities laws and regulations are constantly evolving, and companies must stay informed about changes that could impact their capital-raising efforts. This includes monitoring updates to SEC rules, state-level regulations, and guidance from regulatory authorities. Regularly consulting with legal and compliance professionals can help companies stay compliant and adapt to new requirements as they emerge.

Monitoring Developments That Impact Capital Raising Practices

Changes in securities laws can significantly impact how companies raise capital. For example, the passage of the JOBS Act in 2012 opened new avenues for crowdfunding and general solicitation. Similarly, amendments to Regulation D or Regulation A can affect the exemptions available for private placements. Companies should monitor these developments and adjust their capital-raising strategies accordingly to take advantage of new opportunities or avoid potential compliance pitfalls.

Understanding the Implications of Evolving Regulatory Landscapes

As the regulatory landscape evolves, companies must be prepared to adapt their practices to remain compliant. This may involve updating disclosure documents, revising investor communications, or changing the structure of an offering. Understanding the broader implications of regulatory changes can help companies stay ahead of potential risks and position themselves for success in a dynamic capital-raising environment.

Preparing for Regulatory Reviews

Steps to Prepare for Regulatory Inquiries or Investigations

Preparation is key to successfully navigating regulatory inquiries or investigations. Companies should maintain accurate records of all filings, disclosures, and investor communications because these documents may be requested or subpoenaed. It's also important to conduct regular internal audits to ensure that the company is in compliance with securities laws. Proactive preparation can help companies identify and address potential issues before regulators raise them.

Assembling Necessary Documentation and Records

Companies should have all necessary documentation readily available. This includes offering materials, financial statements, investor communications, and records of compliance with state and federal securities laws. Maintaining well-organized records and making them available quickly to your securities attorney can make an inquiry response more efficient and reduce the risk of delays or additional inquiries from regulators.

Strategies for Responding to Regulatory Inquiries Effectively

If securities regulators raise concerns during an inquiry or as part of an investigation, companies should respond promptly and professionally. It's important to provide clear, detailed responses to any questions or requests for information and to work closely with legal counsel to ensure that all communications are accurate and compliant. Demonstrating a commitment to compliance and cooperation can help resolve issues more quickly and minimize the impact on the company's operations.

Mitigating Enforcement Risks

Identifying Common Enforcement Risks and Pitfalls

Companies raising capital face several common enforcement risks, including failure to provide accurate disclosures, noncompliance with registration requirements, and improper handling of investor funds.

Other risks include general solicitation violations, failure to verify investor accreditation, and misleading marketing materials. Identifying these risks early and taking steps to mitigate them can help companies avoid regulatory scrutiny and enforcement actions.

Proactive Measures to Reduce the Likelihood of Regulatory Violations

To reduce the risk of regulatory violations, companies should implement robust compliance programs that include regular training for management and staff, internal audits, and thorough reviews of all investor communications. Companies should also work closely with legal counsel to ensure that they are following best practices for securities offerings and complying with all applicable laws. Proactive measures such as self-reporting potential violations to regulators can also help mitigate enforcement risks.

Addressing Potential Consequences of Noncompliance

Any noncompliance with securities laws can result in significant consequences, including fines, penalties, cease-and-desist orders, and civil liabilities. In severe cases, companies may face lawsuits from investors or regulatory enforcement actions that can lead to the unwinding of an offering. To mitigate these risks, companies should take a proactive approach to compliance and seek legal counsel if they suspect any violations.

* * * * *

Dealing with federal and state securities regulators is critical to any capital-raising effort. Compliance with federal securities laws and state blue sky laws is essential to ensuring that your offering is legally sound and protects both your business and its investors. Successfully navigating the regulatory landscape requires a proactive approach with clear, accurate disclosures, timely reporting, and open communication with regulators are all key components. By preparing for regulatory reviews and maintaining robust internal compliance practices, you can avoid costly delays and penalties. Continuously involving your securities attorney will not only help you stay ahead of legal requirements but also strengthen your ability to respond to any regulatory inquiries effectively.

CHAPTER **13**

Equity Securities Offerings

Equity securities offerings are a cornerstone of raising capital for businesses of all sizes. Whether a company is issuing common stock, preferred stock, or equity interests in an LLC or LP, understanding the nuances of each type of equity offering is essential for both issuers and investors. This chapter will explore the various types of equity offerings, their unique characteristics, and the legal and regulatory considerations involved in raising capital through equity.

Types of Equity Offerings

Defining Common Stock and Its Characteristics

Common stock represents the most basic form of equity ownership in a corporation. When investors purchase common stock, they gain a stake in the company and are entitled to certain rights such as voting on corporate matters and receiving dividends if declared. Common stockholders are at the bottom of the capital structure, meaning they are the last to receive any assets in the event of liquidation. This higher level of risk is balanced by the potential for substantial gains if the company grows and its stock price appreciates.

Exploring Preferred Stock and Its Benefits

Preferred stock is a type of equity that sits between debt and common stock in a company's capital structure. Preferred stockholders enjoy certain advantages over common stockholders, including priority in dividend payments and liquidation preferences. In some cases, preferred stock may also come with conversion rights allowing holders to convert their shares into common stock under specified conditions. This hybrid nature of preferred stock makes it an attractive option for investors seeking a blend of income (through dividends) and potential capital appreciation.

Understanding Equity Offerings in Limited Liability Companies and Limited Partnerships

Equity offerings in LLCs and LPs differ from those in corporations. Instead of common or preferred stock, investors in LLCs receive membership interests, whereas those in LPs receive partnership interests. These equity interests typically come with different rights and responsibilities compared to corporate stockholders. For example, LLC members may have direct involvement in managing the business, whereas limited partners in an LP have a more passive role. The structure of LLCs and LPs provides flexibility in governance and profit distribution, making them appealing to investors with different goals and risk tolerances.

Common Stock

Key Features and Rights of Common Stockholders

Common stockholders have several key rights, including voting on major corporate decisions such as electing board members, approving mergers, and making other significant changes to the company's structure. Common stockholders are also entitled to dividends, although these payments are typically not guaranteed and depend on the company's profitability and board decisions. The value of common stock is closely tied to the company's financial performance and market conditions, giving stockholders a direct interest in the success of the business.

Discussing Voting Rights and Participation in Company Decisions

Voting rights are a key feature of common stock, allowing shareholders to influence corporate governance. Typically, each share of common stock provides one vote, but companies can issue multiple classes of stock with different voting rights. For example, some companies issue Class A shares with one vote per share and Class B shares with enhanced voting power. These structures allow founders and early investors to retain control of the company while raising capital from outside investors.

Analyzing the Risks and Potential Rewards Associated with Common Stock Investments

Investing in common stock comes with both risks and rewards. Common stockholders are the last to be paid in the event of a company's liquidation, meaning they may receive nothing if the company's assets are insufficient to cover debt and other liabilities. However, the upside potential can be significant if the company grows and its stock price appreciates. For investors with a higher risk tolerance, common stock offers the possibility of substantial capital gains over the long term.

Preferred Stock

Examining the Advantages of Preferred Stock for Investors

Preferred stock offers several advantages over common stock, particularly in terms of risk mitigation and income generation. Preferred stockholders have priority over common stockholders when it comes to receiving dividends and recovering their investment in the event of liquidation. This makes preferred stock a safer option for investors who prioritize income and downside protection. Additionally, preferred stock often comes with fixed dividend payments, providing a reliable income stream for investors.

Differentiating Between Various Classes of Preferred Stock

Not all preferred stock is created equal; there are different classes with varying rights and features. For example, cumulative preferred stock ensures that missed dividend payments accumulate and must be paid in full before common shareholders receive any dividends. Convertible preferred stock allows investors to convert their shares into common stock, typically at a predetermined ratio, offering a potential upside if the company's common stock appreciates in value. Other classes may include participating preferred stock, which allows investors to receive additional dividends if the company performs well.

Highlighting Dividend Preferences and Conversion Options

Dividend preferences are a key feature of preferred stock to ensure that preferred shareholders receive their dividends before any payments are made to common stockholders. Conversion options give investors the flexibility to convert their preferred shares into common stock often at favorable terms. This option is particularly valuable in high-growth companies because it allows preferred shareholders to participate in the appreciation of the company's stock price while still enjoying the benefits of preferred stock.

LLC and LP Interests

Exploring Equity Offerings in the Context of LLCs and LPs

In LLCs, equity is issued in the form of membership interests, whereas investors in LPs receive partnership interests. These forms of equity differ from traditional corporate stock in that they often provide more flexibility in governance and profit distribution. LLC members may be involved in managing the company, whereas LP investors are typically limited to a passive role with general partners managing the business. The flexible structure of LLCs and LPs allows companies to tailor their equity offerings to the needs of both the business and the investors.

Understanding the Unique Structure and Governance of These Entities

LLCs and LPs are governed by operating agreements or partnership agreements that outline the rights and responsibilities of the members or partners. These agreements typically include provisions related to profit sharing, decision-making authority, and the transfer of ownership interests. Unlike corporations where governance is centralized in a board of directors, LLCs and LPs often allow for more decentralized management, particularly in LLCs where members can participate directly in decision-making.

Comparing Investor Rights and Responsibilities in LLC and LP Interests

Investors in LLCs and LPs have different rights and responsibilities than do stockholders in corporations. In LLCs, members may have voting rights and direct involvement in managing the company depending on the structure of the operating agreement. In LPs, limited partners typically have no management authority, whereas general partners assume full responsibility for the business's operations. However, both LLC and LP investors benefit from limited liability meaning they are not personally liable for the company's debts beyond their initial investment.

Considerations for Issuers

Factors Influencing the Choice Between Common and Preferred Stock

When deciding between issuing common or preferred stock, companies must consider several factors, including their capital needs, investor preferences, and long-term goals. Common stock is typically favored by early-stage companies looking to retain control while offering investors the potential for significant upside. Preferred stock is more attractive to investors seeking income and downside protection making it a good option for later-stage companies or those with steady cash flow. Issuers must balance the desire to attract investors with the need to retain flexibility and control over the business.

Balancing Investor Preferences with Company Goals

Investor preferences play a significant role in determining the type of equity offering a company will pursue. Some investors may prioritize voting rights and control, making common stock more appealing, whereas others may seek the security of preferred dividends and liquidation preferences. Companies must carefully consider how to structure their offerings to meet investor demand without sacrificing their strategic objectives.

Addressing Legal and Regulatory Requirements for Equity Offerings

Issuing equity securities requires compliance with federal and state securities laws, including registration requirements or exemptions under Regulation D, Regulation A, or other SEC rules. Companies must also provide investors with adequate disclosures including information about the risks associated with the investment and the terms of the offering. Working with experienced legal counsel is essential to ensure that the offering complies with all applicable regulations.

Investor Perspectives

Evaluating the Appeal of Different Equity Offerings to Investors

Different types of equity offerings appeal to different types of investors. For example, risk-tolerant investors may prefer common stock because of its potential for high returns, whereas income-focused investors may favor preferred stock for its stable dividend payments. LLC and LP interests may appeal to investors looking for direct involvement in management or more flexible profit-sharing arrangements. Understanding the preferences and risk tolerances of potential investors is key to structuring an equity offering that attracts the right type of capital.

Weighing Risk and Return Factors in Common, Preferred, and Partnership Interests

Each type of equity offers a different risk–return profile. Common stock is typically higher risk but offers the potential for significant capital appreciation. Preferred stock provides more stability with regular dividend payments and priority in liquidation but less potential for growth. LLC and LP interests offer flexibility and potentially higher returns but with more complexity in governance and profit distribution. Investors must carefully weigh these factors when deciding where to allocate their capital.

Strategies for Diversifying a Portfolio with Different Equity Investments

Diversifying a portfolio with different types of equity investments can help investors balance risk and return. By investing in a mix of common stock, preferred stock, and LLC or LP interests, investors can gain exposure to high-growth opportunities while securing more stable income streams. This diversified approach helps mitigate risk and provides more consistent returns over time.

Valuation and Pricing

Determining Valuation Methodologies for Equity Offerings

Valuing equity offerings is critical in the capital-raising process. Common valuation methodologies include DCF analysis, comparable company analysis, and precedent transactions. Each method provides a different perspective on the company's value, and companies often use a combination of these approaches to determine a fair price for their equity offerings.

Pricing Considerations for Common and Preferred Stock

Pricing common and preferred stock involves balancing the company's valuation with investor demand. Common stock is typically priced based on the company's current and projected financial performance, whereas preferred stock may be priced higher because of its dividend payments and liquidation preferences. Issuers must also consider factors such as dilution and anti-dilution provisions, which can affect the value of the equity over time.

Factors Influencing the Pricing of LLC and LP Interests

The pricing of LLC and LP interests is influenced by factors such as the company's revenue, profit margins, and growth potential as well as the terms of the operating or partnership agreement. Because LLCs and LPs offer more flexibility in profit distribution and governance, investors may be willing to pay a premium for interests that provide greater involvement in decision-making or higher returns. However, the lack of liquidity in these types of investments can also impact pricing because investors may require a discount to compensate for the reduced ability to exit their investment.

Regulatory Compliance

Discussing Legal and Regulatory Requirements for Equity Offerings

Equity offerings are subject to a wide range of legal and regulatory requirements, including compliance with federal securities laws, state blue sky laws, and disclosure obligations. Companies must ensure that their offerings comply with SEC rules such as Regulation D or Regulation A and that they provide investors with accurate and complete information about the risks and rewards associated with the investment. Noncompliance can result in penalties, fines, or legal liabilities.

Compliance with Securities Laws and Disclosure Obligations

To comply with securities laws, companies must provide adequate disclosures to investors including information about the company's financial condition, management team, business operations, and risk factors. These disclosures are typically made through a prospectus or PPM, depending on the type of offering. Companies must also ensure that they meet any state-level registration or exemption requirements and that they verify investor accreditation where required.

Compliance Considerations Specific to LLC and LP Interests

LLC and LP interests are subject to different compliance requirements than corporate stock offerings. These interests are often sold through private placements, which may be exempt from SEC registration under Regulation D. However, companies must still comply with state blue sky laws and provide investors with adequate disclosures. Additionally, the terms of the operating or partnership agreement must be carefully drafted to ensure compliance with securities laws and to protect both the company and its investors.

* * * * *

Choosing the right type of equity offering is a critical decision that will have long-term implications for your business. Whether issuing common stock, preferred stock, or equity interests in an LLC or LP, each option comes with its own set of opportunities and responsibilities for both issuers and investors. Balancing the needs of your company with the expectations of investors is essential to structuring an effective capital raise. As you explore your options, consulting with experienced securities counsel will ensure that your offering is compliant with legal requirements and that the terms align with your business goals. By thoughtfully structuring your equity offering, you can attract the right investors while positioning your company for sustainable growth.

CHAPTER 14

Debt Securities Offerings

Debt securities are crucial in corporate finance, offering companies a way to raise capital without diluting ownership and providing investors with a fixed-income investment. In this chapter, we'll explore the types of debt securities, the reasons companies issue them, and how they are valued and priced. We will also examine the risks and rewards for investors, giving both issuers and investors the insights they need to understand debt securities offerings.

Types of Debt Securities

Defining Various Debt Securities (e.g., Notes, Bonds, Debentures)

Debt securities are financial instruments issued by companies, governments, or other entities to raise capital. The most common types of debt securities include notes, bonds, and debentures.

- Notes are short- to medium-term debt instruments, typically maturing within five years.

- Bonds are longer-term securities with maturities ranging from five to 30 years or more. Bonds often pay periodic interest known as coupons.
- Debentures are unsecured bonds that are not backed by specific assets but by the issuer's creditworthiness.

Each type of debt security comes with specific terms such as maturity date, interest payments, and repayment conditions, giving issuers flexibility in structuring their financing.

Characteristics and Features of Each Type

The key features of debt securities include the maturity date, interest (or coupon) rate, and face value (the amount to be repaid at maturity). Debt securities can be structured to pay fixed or variable interest rates. Investors are compensated for the time value of money and the risk of default through interest payments. The repayment terms, collateral (if any), and creditworthiness of the issuer are also important characteristics that affect the value and risk of the security.

Differentiating Between Secured and Unsecured Debt Securities

A key distinction between debt securities is whether they are secured or unsecured.

- Secured debt securities are backed by specific assets such as real estate or equipment serving as collateral. If the issuer defaults, the assets can be sold to repay investors. Secured bonds such as mortgage-backed securities are examples of this type.
- Unsecured debt securities such as debentures are not backed by specific collateral. Instead, they are based solely on the issuer's creditworthiness. Investors in unsecured debt take on more risk but may receive higher yields to compensate for that risk.

Issuer's Perspective

Why Companies Issue Debt Securities

Companies issue debt securities for various reasons, including raising capital for expansion, funding new projects, or refinancing existing debt. Unlike equity financing, issuing debt does not dilute ownership, allowing founders and shareholders to retain control. Debt securities also provide predictable costs in the form of interest payments, which can be easier to manage than the variability of issuing equity.

Understanding the Advantages and Considerations for Issuers

The advantages of issuing debt securities include maintaining ownership control, accessing large amounts of capital, and potentially lowering the company's overall cost of capital. Interest payments on debt are tax-deductible for a further financial benefit. However, companies must carefully manage the risks associated with debt, including the obligation to make regular interest payments regardless of business performance. Failure to meet these obligations can lead to default and financial distress, particularly with secured debt where assets are at stake.

Addressing Legal and Regulatory Requirements for Debt Offerings

Issuing debt securities requires compliance with federal and state securities regulations. Companies must ensure that their offerings comply with the Securities Act of 1933 and, if applicable, state blue sky laws. Many debt offerings are conducted under exemptions from registration such as Regulation D for private placements. However, public debt offerings require filing a registration statement with the SEC. Issuers must also disclose material information about their financial condition and the terms of the offering to potential investors. Legal counsel plays a critical role in ensuring that debt offerings meet all regulatory requirements.

Investor's Perspective

Evaluating the Appeal of Debt Securities to Investors

Debt securities are attractive to investors seeking steady, predictable income. Unlike equity investments, which can fluctuate in value, debt securities provide fixed payments over a specified period. Bonds, notes, and debentures are often viewed as lower-risk investments, especially if they are issued by creditworthy companies or secured by collateral. Debt securities can also provide diversification within an investment portfolio to balance out riskier equity holdings.

Risks and Rewards of Debt Investments

While debt securities offer stability, they have risks. The primary risk is default risk or the risk that the issuer will be unable to meet its interest or principal payments. This risk is particularly high for unsecured debt, where investors have no claim to specific assets. Interest rate risk is another factor because rising interest rates can reduce the market value of fixed-rate debt securities. However, for risk-averse investors, the fixed income and higher priority in liquidation compared to equity holders make debt securities an appealing option.

Diversifying Investment Portfolios with Debt Securities

Including debt securities in a diversified portfolio helps reduce overall risk by providing a counterbalance to more volatile equity investments. For example, during periods of stock market downturns, the fixed-interest payments from bonds or notes can provide stability and cash flow.

Investors can diversify further by investing in a mix of short-, medium-, and long-term debt as well as in both secured and unsecured instruments to spread risk across different issuers and maturity profiles.

Valuation and Pricing

Determining Valuation Methodologies for Debt Securities

The value of a debt security is primarily determined by its interest rate and maturity date and the issuer's creditworthiness. The present value of the expected cash flows (interest payments and the repayment of principal) is calculated using a discount rate that reflects the risk of the security. Credit ratings from agencies such as Moody's or S&P are also critical in determining the value of debt securities because higher-rated securities are seen as lower risk and therefore have lower yields.

Pricing Considerations for Notes, Bonds, and Debentures

Pricing debt securities involves assessing the coupon rate relative to prevailing interest rates in the market. When a bond's coupon rate is higher than current market rates, the bond will trade at a premium (above its face value). Conversely, if market interest rates rise above the coupon rate, the bond will trade at a discount (below its face value). Other factors influencing pricing include the time to maturity, inflation expectations, and the liquidity of the bond in the secondary market.

Factors Influencing Interest Rates and Yields

Several factors influence the interest rates and yields of debt securities, including macroeconomic conditions, inflation rates, and central bank policies. A company's credit risk, the likelihood that it will default on its debt obligations, also plays a significant role. Investors demand higher yields for debt securities with higher credit risk to compensate for the potential loss. Secured debt typically offers lower yields than unsecured debt because of the reduced risk associated with the collateral.

* * * * *

Structuring a debt securities offering requires careful consideration of both the benefits and risks involved. Debt instruments can provide companies with a reliable source of capital while allowing them to maintain ownership control, but they also come with obligations such as regular interest payments and eventual repayment of the principal. Understanding the distinctions between secured and unsecured debt as well as the importance of pricing and valuation is key to ensuring a successful offering. Throughout this process, working closely with experienced securities counsel is essential to navigating the complex regulatory requirements and ensuring that the terms are favorable both to your business and to your investors. By taking the time to structure your debt offering properly, you can raise the necessary capital to fuel growth while protecting your company's long-term interests.

CHAPTER **15**

Investment Contracts, Tokens, Special Purpose Entities, and Alternative Securities

As the capital-raising landscape evolves, businesses and investors have a growing number of alternative securities to consider beyond traditional stocks and bonds. This chapter explores investment contracts, tokens, special purpose entities (SPEs), and other nontraditional securities offering insights into their structure, regulatory frameworks, and investor considerations. Understanding these alternative securities is crucial for both issuers and investors looking to diversify their strategies and navigate the complexities of modern financial markets.

Understanding Investment Contracts

Defining Investment Contracts and Their Characteristics

An investment contract is a type of security where an individual invests money in a common enterprise with the expectation of earning profits primarily from the efforts of others. Investment contracts can take many forms, including limited partnerships, real estate investment agreements, and certain crowdfunding arrangements. The broad definition allows for a variety of financial products to be classified as investment contracts.

Regulatory Framework and Howey Test

The determination of whether an arrangement constitutes an investment contract is governed by what has become known as the "Howey" Test, a legal framework established by the US Supreme Court (*SEC v. W.J. Howey Co.*, 328 US 293 [1946]). Under this test, an arrangement is considered an investment contract if it involves an investment of money in a common enterprise with the expectation of profits that is primarily generated by the efforts of others.

The Howey Test remains the cornerstone of US securities law for determining whether an offering must comply with federal securities regulations, making it essential for issuers of nontraditional securities to understand its application.

Examples of Investment Contracts in Practice

Investment contracts are commonly used in areas like real estate syndications, certain types of joint ventures, and token offerings that may fall under the definition of securities. For example, real estate developers often raise capital by offering fractional ownership interests in properties, where investors expect returns based on the developer's efforts. Similarly, some token offerings may be classified as investment contracts if they meet the criteria of the Howey Test.

Token Offerings (Tokenization)

What Are Tokens and Tokenization?

Tokens represent digital assets issued on blockchain platforms. "Tokenization" refers to the process of converting physical or financial assets such as real estate, stocks, or bonds into digital tokens. These tokens can be bought, sold, and traded on digital platforms, offering a new way for businesses to raise capital and for investors to access a broader range of assets.

Types of Tokens: Security Tokens, Utility Tokens, and More

There are several types of tokens used in capital raising.

- Security tokens, which represent ownership in an asset or company, are regulated as securities under federal law. These tokens offer equity-like benefits and are subject to securities regulations.
- Utility tokens provide access to a product or service and are not typically considered securities. However, if utility tokens are marketed with the expectation of profits, they may be subject to securities laws.
- Non-fungible tokens are unique digital assets that represent ownership of a specific item, such as artwork or intellectual property.

Benefits and Challenges of Token Offerings

Token offerings allow companies to raise capital quickly and efficiently by tapping into global investor pools. Tokens offer the potential for increased liquidity, transparency, and accessibility compared to traditional securities. However, the regulatory landscape for token offerings is complex and varies by jurisdiction. Issuers must navigate legal uncertainties, particularly around whether a token offering qualifies as a securities offering subject to SEC regulations.

Special Purpose Entities

What Are SPEs and Their Purpose?

A SPE is a legal entity created for a specific, narrow purpose often to isolate financial risk or raise capital for a specific project. SPEs are commonly used in structured finance transactions, such as asset-backed securities, where the SPE holds the underlying assets and issues securities backed by them. SPEs help companies manage risk and protect assets while raising capital in a structured and isolated manner.

Role of SPEs in Structured Finance and Capital Raising

SPEs play a critical role in securitization and other complex financing structures. By holding specific assets or projects in an SPE, the parent company can raise capital without exposing its entire balance sheet to risk. For example, in a mortgage-backed security, the mortgages are transferred to an SPE that then issues bonds backed by the income from the mortgages. This allows the parent company to raise capital while limiting its risk exposure.

Legal and Regulatory Considerations for SPEs

While SPEs offer significant benefits, they are also subject to strict legal and regulatory scrutiny. SPEs must comply with securities regulations if they issue securities to investors, and there are legal requirements to ensure that the SPE operates independently from the parent company. Additionally, SPEs have faced criticism in cases where they have been used to hide liabilities or engage in off-balance-sheet financing, leading to increased regulatory oversight.

Crowdfunding and Crowdsourcing

Exploring Crowdfunding Models (Equity Crowdfunding, Rewards-Based, Donation-Based)

Crowdfunding allows companies to raise capital by collecting small investments from a large number of individuals often through online platforms. The most common types of crowdfunding include the following:

- Equity crowdfunding, where investors receive ownership shares in the company
- Rewards-based crowdfunding, where backers receive nonfinancial rewards, such as early access to a product
- Donation-based crowdfunding, where contributors donate money to a cause without expecting a financial return

Using Crowdsourcing for Fundraising and Idea Generation

Beyond raising capital, companies can use crowdsourcing to generate ideas, test products, and engage with their community. By leveraging the power of a large, distributed group of people, companies can tap into collective creativity and innovation, enhancing their fundraising efforts and improving their product development process.

Regulatory Landscape for Crowdfunding

Equity crowdfunding is regulated by the SEC, particularly under Reg CF, which allows companies to raise up to $5 million from both accredited and non-accredited investors. Issuers must comply with specific disclosure requirements, including filing offering documents with the SEC and providing detailed information about the company and the offering. Crowdfunding platforms must also be registered with the SEC and FINRA.

Digital Securities and Blockchain

How Blockchain Technology Is Revolutionizing Securities Issuance

Blockchain technology has transformed the issuance and trading of securities by providing a decentralized, transparent, and secure platform for transactions. Digital securities (i.e., security tokens) can be issued and traded on blockchain platforms, enabling faster settlement times, lower transaction costs, and improved liquidity compared to traditional securities markets.

Benefits of Digital Securities

Digital securities offer several advantages, including increased transparency, reduced intermediaries, and greater accessibility for global investors. Blockchain's distributed ledger ensures that all transactions are securely recorded and easily auditable, reducing the risk of fraud. Digital securities can also be fractionalized, allowing investors to purchase smaller portions of high-value assets, such as real estate or fine art.

Legal and Compliance Aspects of Digital Securities

Issuers of digital securities must navigate a complex regulatory landscape. In the US, digital securities are treated as securities under federal law, meaning they are subject to the same regulations as traditional securities. This includes registration requirements under the Securities Act of 1933, unless the offering qualifies for an exemption such as Regulation D. Compliance with anti-money laundering and know-your-customer regulations is also critical in digital securities offerings.

Hybrid Securities

Understanding Hybrid Securities That Combine Traditional and Alternative Elements

Hybrid securities blend the characteristics of both debt and equity instruments, providing investors with a mix of fixed income and potential capital appreciation. Examples of hybrid securities include convertible bonds, which can be converted into equity at a future date, and preferred shares that offer fixed dividends but may also provide the opportunity for conversion into common stock. Hybrid securities allow companies to tailor their offerings to meet both their capital needs and investor demand.

Successful Hybrid Securities Offerings

Many companies have successfully raised capital through hybrid securities offerings. For instance, high-growth companies have used convertible bonds to raise debt capital with the potential for equity conversion, offering investors downside protection with an opportunity for upside participation. Preferred stock offerings are another example, where companies provide investors with income through fixed dividends while retaining flexibility for future equity conversion.

Evaluating the Investor Appeal of Hybrid Instruments

Hybrid securities appeal to investors seeking a balance between income and growth potential. They offer fixed returns through dividends or interest payments while providing the potential for capital appreciation through conversion options. These instruments can serve as a middle ground for investors who want more security than equity investments but are willing to take on more risk than traditional debt.

Regulatory Compliance and Challenges

Navigating the Complex Regulatory Environment for Nontraditional Securities

The regulatory environment for alternative securities, such as tokens and hybrid securities, is complex and rapidly evolving. Companies issuing these securities must ensure compliance with both federal and state securities laws, including the Securities Act of 1933, the Securities Exchange Act of 1934, and state blue sky laws. For token offerings and digital securities, additional considerations around blockchain regulation and investor protection are critical.

Compliance with Securities Laws and Exemptions

Issuers of alternative securities often rely on exemptions from SEC registration such as Regulation D (for private placements) or Regulation A (for smaller public offerings). These exemptions provide flexibility but come with their own compliance obligations, including investor accreditation requirements and disclosure mandates. Navigating these exemptions requires a thorough understanding of securities laws and ongoing consultation with legal counsel.

Challenges and Potential Risks in the Evolving Regulatory Landscape

As the regulatory environment for alternative securities continues to evolve, issuers face potential risks, including increased scrutiny from regulators, evolving legal interpretations, and changing compliance requirements. Companies must remain vigilant in monitoring regulatory developments and adapting their practices to mitigate potential risks.

Investor Considerations

Perspectives of Investors in Nontraditional Securities

Investors in alternative securities such as tokens, hybrid instruments, and investment contracts must carefully assess the risks and rewards of these investments. Nontraditional securities often come with higher risks due to regulatory uncertainty, limited liquidity, and evolving market conditions. However, they also offer unique opportunities for diversification and higher returns, particularly in emerging markets like blockchain and tokenization.

Risk Assessment and Due Diligence

Before investing in nontraditional securities, investors must conduct thorough due diligence including assessing the issuer's financial health, understanding the terms of the offering, and evaluating the regulatory risks. Investors should also consider the liquidity of the investment because many alternative securities may have limited secondary markets.

Strategies for Diversifying Portfolios with Alternative Investments

Incorporating alternative securities into a diversified portfolio can help investors balance risk and reward. By investing in a mix of traditional stocks and bonds alongside tokens, hybrid securities, and other nontraditional assets, investors can reduce their exposure to market volatility and take advantage of emerging investment opportunities.

* * * * *

Navigating the world of alternative securities, whether through investment contracts, token offerings, or special purpose entities, requires a thorough understanding of their unique structures and regulatory challenges. Each option presents exciting opportunities for innovation and capital raising, but these opportunities come with significant legal and compliance responsibilities. As financial markets evolve, it is crucial to stay informed of the shifting regulatory landscape and engage with experienced legal counsel to ensure that your offerings remain compliant. By approaching these alternatives with careful planning and expert advice, you can tap into emerging financial tools while safeguarding both your business and your investors.

CHAPTER **16**

Raising Capital with Confidence

Raising capital is one of the most critical and complex steps for any entrepreneur or business. Throughout this book, we've explored the diverse methods and strategies available for raising capital from private placements and public offerings to cutting-edge options like token offerings and crowdfunding. Each chapter has provided an in-depth look at the instruments, regulatory frameworks, and considerations involved in choosing the right path for your business.

Summarizing the Major Points

The capital-raising landscape is dynamic and multifaceted. Here are the key takeaways every entrepreneur should keep in mind as they embark on their fundraising journey:

- **Understand your options:** There are numerous ways to raise capital, each with its own advantages, challenges, and legal implications. Whether you opt for equity offerings, debt securities, or alternative instruments like tokens or special purpose entities, understanding the structure and trade-offs of each method is essential. Carefully assess the needs of your business, the preferences of your investors, and your long-term goals to determine which method aligns best.

- **Know your investors:** Different capital-raising strategies attract different types of investors. High-risk, high-reward options like common stock will appeal to risk-tolerant investors, whereas income-focused investors may prefer safer investments like preferred stock or debt securities. Crowdfunding opens the door to a broader pool of investors including non-accredited participants. Understanding the needs and expectations of your target investors can help you structure an offering that resonates with them.

- **Remember that compliance is key:** Whether raising capital through a public offering or a private placement, you must remember that strict adherence to federal and state securities regulations is crucial. Compliance with securities laws, including the Securities Act of 1933, the Securities Exchange Act of 1934, and state blue sky laws cannot be overlooked. Noncompliance can lead to severe penalties, legal action, and reputational damage. This is especially true for newer fundraising methods like tokenization and digital securities, where the regulatory framework is still evolving.

- **Ensure transparency in disclosure:** One of the cornerstones of securities law is full and fair disclosure. Investors must be given clear, accurate, and comprehensive information about your business and the terms of the offering. Whether it's a PPM for a private offering or a prospectus for a public offering, your disclosure documents must present a balanced view of risks and opportunities and comply with all regulatory requirements.

- **Consider the costs:** Raising capital has its costs. Public offerings can be expensive and time-consuming with substantial fees for legal, accounting, and underwriting services. Private placements, while more streamlined, also come with costs related to legal compliance and investor due diligence. Even newer methods like crowdfunding require investment in marketing and regulatory filings. Understanding these costs ahead of time will help you plan your capital-raising strategy more effectively.

- **Evaluate Liquidity and Exit Strategies:** Liquidity is a key concern for both you and your investors. Public offerings offer immediate liquidity through stock exchanges, but they come with greater regulatory burdens and market volatility. Private offerings provide more flexibility but less liquidity. Hybrid and alternative securities, such as convertible notes or tokens, offer unique exit strategies but also come with their own complexities. It's important to align your liquidity strategy with the needs of your investors and the future plans of your company.

The Importance of Engaging a Seasoned Securities Attorney

If there is one takeaway that cannot be overstated, it is to always engage a seasoned securities attorney or law firm before embarking on your capital-raising efforts. The capital-raising process is fraught with legal complexities and potential pitfalls that could derail your business if not handled properly. A securities attorney will help you with many issues.

- **Navigate regulatory compliance:** An attorney will ensure that your offering is structured in accordance with federal and state securities laws, helping you avoid costly mistakes that could lead to regulatory penalties or legal action.
- **Draft and review key documents:** From PPMs to subscription agreements and offering circulars, your attorney will help you prepare the legal documents needed to protect both your company and your investors. They will also ensure that these documents contain all required disclosures and meet regulatory standards.
- **Manage investor relationships:** Securities attorneys can provide guidance on managing relationships with investors, including issues related to investor rights, voting power, and exit strategies. This

ensures that you strike the right balance between raising capital and maintaining control of your business.

- **Stay ahead of regulatory changes:** The regulatory landscape for capital raising is constantly evolving, especially with new developments in areas like digital securities and token offerings. An experienced attorney will keep you informed of changes that could impact your fundraising strategy and ensure that you remain compliant.

Raising capital is a transformative step for any business, and when done right, it can fuel your growth and set you on the path to long-term success. However, it's a journey that requires careful planning, deep understanding of the financial and regulatory landscape, and expert legal guidance. By being informed, diligent, and proactive and seeking the support of a seasoned securities attorney, you can navigate the complexities of capital raising with confidence.

This book has hopefully equipped you with the knowledge and tools to make informed decisions. Now, as you move forward in your capital-raising journey, remember that success comes from being prepared, understanding your investors, and adhering to the rules that protect them and your business.

Armed with the right knowledge, strategic insights, and legal guidance, raising capital can be an exciting, transformative step toward realizing your business's full potential.

Thank you for investing your time in reading this book and for taking the initiative to better understand this vital aspect of your business. As you apply the ideas and strategies outlined in this book, I want to personally wish you the best of luck on your journey.

I would love to hear how these concepts have worked for you. Feel free to reach out to me at any time. Your journey is inspiring, and I'd welcome your feedback and updates as you raise capital with confidence.

* * * * *

ABOUT THE AUTHOR

Darin H. Mangum, Esq., is in his 25th year as managing partner of Mangum & Associates PC, a specialized boutique securities law firm with clients worldwide. Mangum & Associates PC focuses on private placement offerings conducted under Regulation D as well as public offerings under Regulation A and other US federal and state and international securities laws. Darin's clients include private investment companies; real estate syndicators; real estate acquisition and development projects; private lending funds; private equity funds; VC funds; hedge funds; blockchain-related and cryptocurrency token issuers; FINRA broker/dealers and SEC-registered investment advisory firms; technology start-ups; EB5 sponsors and regional investment centers; opportunity zone funds; and oil, gas, alternative energy and mining ventures. Darin also currently serves as CEO of ZuLoo, Inc., a benefit corporation ("ZuLoo") that is focused on finding innovative solutions to the global sanitation crisis through the power of social enterprise. He also serves on the board of directors for ZuLoo Humanitarian, a nonprofit charitable organization affiliated with ZuLoo, which provides toilets, hygiene, clean water, and sanitation to people who are underserved. Darin received his law degree from Brigham Young University in 1999 and is a member of the State Bar of Texas and the Utah State Bar.

To connect with Darin's law firm,
please use the following contact information:

MANGUM & ASSOCIATES PC
America's Premier Securities Law Firm ™
Toll-Free: +1.888.685.8676
Direct/Text: +1.801.787.9072
Email: *darin@mangum.law*
Web: *www.mangum.law*

Got a question for Darin?
Chat with him now by scanning this QR code:

or go to *https://darinmangum.ai/*